EAT
IN PEACE
TO
LIVE
IN PEACE

YOUR HANDBOOK
for VITALITY

CHARLOTTE KIKEL, MS

3 Dragons 8 an Ox

Published by 3 Dragons & an Ox
Copyright © 2018 by Charlotte Kikel

To contact the author, visit www.charlottekikel.com

Cover and text design by Sheila Parr
Cover image © Shutterstock / alevtina

Paperback ISBN: 978-0-9996045-1-9
Ebook ISBN: 978-0-9996045-2-6

Printed in the United States of America
First Edition

CONTENTS

This book is dedicated to

My dad, who said, "Charlotte, walk like you know
where you're going and talk like you know
what you're talking about."
(Hey, Dad, thanks for the good advice. I don't
have to pretend anymore! Miss you.)

My mom. I couldn't have written this book without you.
You are not a burden. You are a gift to our family, and
this book is 100% dedicated to you.

My husband. Thanks for not going anywhere. Love. Love.

And our son. So glad you chose us.

INTRODUCTION

*"Truth is like the sun. You can shut it out for
a while, but it ain't goin' away."*

—ELVIS PRESLEY

I'm going to ask you to do something strange. I want you to think about what it was like in the comfort of your mother's womb. All cozy and warm. You didn't know where you ended and your mother began. You were cared for and life was wonderful. It was the epitome of oneness.

But it was also dark and constrained in that lovely uterus, and you started to get restless. "I'm so comfortable here, but I think there's something more out there!"

Around the 9-month mark, you had outgrown this living arrangement, and you sent a message to your mother's body that you were ready to come out. And her sole job was to surrender to the wisdom of the birthing process, while you traveled down the vaginal canal.

You didn't know what you were in for, did you? All of a sudden you had to fit through this really tight space. There were times when you thought you couldn't do it, but your body worked with you, and mom helped.

Being born hurt! Moving into the light is hard work! You can't turn back now!

Can you see the analogy here? Healing is like being born again, and requires that you call upon the same intense energy that it took for you to come into this world. Getting sick is your body signaling that something isn't working. Something has to die in order for you to truly live. You have to leave something behind in this process. You have to face yourself and ask the question: Am I going to stay here in this world that I know, even if I can't move, or am I going to leave this place that I call home, and burst forth into something new?

Obviously, I can't speak for you, but for me, there is one word and one word only that comes to mind when I think what would have propelled me down and out of the vaginal canal. If I could have talked while coming into this world, what would I have said?

Fuuuuuuuuuuuuuuck!

This is the word that carries me through the pain of being alive.

In addition to all the other advice in this book, fuck is one of my secrets to vitality.

Fuck moves me forward in life.

Fuck is a word of power.

Fuck says enough is enough.

When your energy gets stagnant and you suffer from dis-ease, fuck gets you unstuck.

Fuck is more than a word of power; it is a word of movement.

Saying fuck is what got me off the bathroom floor, crying, in a chronic inflammatory-cascade from hell in 2008.

Fuck is what kept me engaged in life when I didn't feel like living. It helped me continue to look for answers. I knew there was more to life than what I was experiencing.

Fuck mobilizes the forces within me. Saying fuck motivates me to take that next step.

The other day I was talking to a dear friend, and she said, "Yeah, saying fuck just helps me feel better. It's, like, a release of tension. I. Just. Feel. Better."

If a one-syllable word can help you feel like this, I say, "Use it!"

Saying fuck removes the façade that everything is ok when it's not.

Fuck takes all of these images of wellness, green drinks, yoga, happiness and joy, and makes life real again.

I was listening to a parenting show a few years ago, and the guest speaking about feeding kids healthy foods (and the lack thereof) said, "I love making people angry, because angry people do something!"

Yes. Appropriate anger has a purpose. And we have access to an amazing word that both expresses anger AND creates movement.

Yet so many people in the health and wellness movement frown on expressing anger. They try to convince us that the problem is our perspective. But you know what? As my aunt used to say, "Life is a puckered asshole." And she was right. Life just sucks sometimes. And thinking differently about it doesn't change that. You know what does change it? Getting angry. So I say, embrace your anger. Take that fuck and channel it into meaningful action.

When I was birthing my child, I started saying fuck in very weird ways. My midwife very gently said to me, "Charlotte, take that fuck and turn it into a push."

That's what I am talking about here. Take that fuck and birth something new into the world.

Take what many believe to be vulgar and profane and turn it into something holy and profound.

The word fuck humbles me, just like Nature. It is transformational language that is as powerful as eating a good meal and getting a good night's sleep. And it's FREE and always available to you!

Fuck is dynamic. It is vital and alive. It isn't all about anger and boundaries. It can express just about anything, and expressing your self is healing.

People eat themselves into obesity because they suppress their anxiety and anger about life. Deal with your stress instead of smothering your negative feelings with food.

Suffer more. Suppress less.

Saying fuck is an internal release valve.

This is what I want you to know: When you go to that yoga class or juice shop or workshop, or buy that motivational book, and still feel like something is off—like, why is everyone so fucking happy, and I'm not?—know that what you sense is real. Under all the smiles and "just think positive" advice is often a glorification of youth and a denial of death.

Eat this way and live this way and nothing bad will happen to you.

That's bullshit.

Remember: life is a puckered asshole.

We are going to die, and if you get old and chubby with grey hair, consider yourself lucky. Vitality is about knowing that, and being alive while you are here.

Too often, the wellness movement encourages us to feel positive emotions at the exclusion of the negative ones. People don't know what to do with their anger and grief, so they stuff it down, often over-eating and even over-exercising to manage their feelings.

I believe part of the solution is embracing the word fuck in all of its glory.

And so it goes with life. Painful events have the capability to transform us if we don't escape them with a bottle of wine and cupcakes.

Case in point: when I was writing this book, I worked with a lot of wonderful people. One of my editors said, "Charlotte, it sounds like you're saying that if a person does these four things that they will get better. Is that right?"

Upon reading this at my computer, I wanted to pull my hair out and scream, "Fuck no! That is not what I'm saying!"

Why I wrote this book

I wrote this book to honor the divine feminine and the spiral nature of life. Everything cycles. The ups and downs are inherent within each and every day, throughout the seasons, and over the years of your life.

This is particularly evident in the healing process, where straight lines do not exist. We go backwards, we go forwards, and sometimes even sideways, and there is a lot of confusion before there is clarity.

And sometimes the wellness industry doesn't help. One of the biggest lies it sells us is the idea that at some point in the future everything will be ok. If you eat this way, your life will be perfect. If you do this cleanse, you'll lose 20 pounds. If you do this exercise, your body will be perfect. If you take this supplement, all your problems will go away. No, it won't. Life will just keep life-ing.

Sure, some tools may improve your emotional and

physical strength to cope with stress, but that's pretty much the extent of it.

In addition, linear thinking and the results of double-blind controlled studies rarely pave the way for personal vitality. Their certainty is appealing, but not real.

The reality is that there are no guarantees. What works for you and what works for me may look very different, and sometimes, nothing may work.

After I became sick and went to nutrition school in California, I got so tired of seeing images of skinny, happy people going to yoga class with green smoothies in their hands. While there is nothing wrong with yoga, green drinks, and happy people, they weren't appealing to me, and these images were in stark contrast to my healing journey, which wasn't very pretty.

When I started to improve my dietary and lifestyle choices, I was depressed, angry, anxious, and exhausted. The inflammation in my body made me puffy. I couldn't watch a movie without falling asleep. As you will read shortly, I was a hot mess.

But I kept going. I kept asking for help. I kept learning and studying. I began to trust my body, and it was so worth it. I see so many people give up when their healing process fails to match the beautiful images presented by the wellness movement. Despite the hardships I encountered, I knew deeply that I was right where I needed to be, so I stayed on course. I want you to have that deep knowing of what is right and good in your life, even when things are going to hell in a hand-basket.

If you're picking up this book, it's likely you've been trying to heal yourself for a long time. Maybe you have a chronic inflammatory disease, like diabetes or one of the eighty autoimmune diseases that now exist. Maybe you have asthma, chronic headaches, digestive and sleep disturbances, aching muscles, or anxiety and depression, as I did.

Or maybe you are between 30 and 40 years of age, and your body just isn't like it used to be. Strange things are happening and you can't figure out why.

Whatever your situation, I want you to consider that most of us are led to look for healing in the wrong places. We have been told to trust the person in the white coat and the numbers on our blood work at the expense of listening to our bodies. So we go from doctor to doctor to doctor, hoping that this time, he or she will listen instead of relying exclusively on lab results, and work with us to solve the mystery of what ails us.

We're giving too much of our power away.

We're not the only ones guilty of not listening.

We wouldn't need doctors to tell us what's wrong if we would just pay attention to what our bodies are telling us.

Many clients show up in my office carrying file folders filled with the results of hundreds, even thousands, of dollars' worth of tests, begging me to figure out what's wrong. Yet when I ask them two questions—"What did you eat for breakfast this morning? And when did you go to bed last night?"—they shift uncomfortably in their chairs. Their answer is usually something like, "Well, I didn't have time to eat this morning, and I went to bed a little after midnight."

Let's start there. Please. Don't let all the modern technology distract you from the basics of what creates life.

I didn't heal by spending tons of money on fancy tests or by taking pharmaceutical drugs or looking at my genes.

This isn't a sexy book filled with the latest wellness technologies or scientific studies.

This is a book about blood, sweat, tears, and trust.

Sometimes the pain of healing is greater than the pain of being sick. That's the turd in the punchbowl that I want to talk about with you.

Often the most painful and uncomfortable moments in life come as a result of the healing process. These are periods of deep transformation. Instead of working to make them go away, we need to step fully into them.

After all, true wellness is not only the absence of disease; it is also the ability to cope when you hurt and the willingness to embrace uncertainty.

And it doesn't matter what you suffer from. The underlying causes are the same. In the words of Hippocrates, the father of Western medicine, "It is more important to know what sort of person has a disease than to know what sort of disease a person has."

The only question you need to be asking is this: what is my body adapting to? My hope is that as you read this book, you will be able to answer this question very clearly and then move into right action. Not because I told you to, but because you have a new understanding of your situation, and WANT to do something different!

You don't need another book filled with facts. That's

what the Internet is for these days. I want to give you a new way to think about food, your body, and your place in this world.

This book is about discovering what makes your body sing, because when you honor that and sing your unique song, you won't be able to contain yourself. Your vitality will be overflowing.

What is vitality?

I define vitality as a spiritual expression of health.

It is about living with purpose and intention.

We can't talk about vitality without talking about Spirit. Please use whatever word works for you—God, Universe, Divine Being, Allah, etc. Spirit is what I'm most comfortable with.

Spirit isn't something outside of us. It is inside us and all around us. It is the energy moving through you that animates you, without which you would be a useless pile of mush on the floor.

Spirit connects everything.

Some people seek this connection to Spirit in nature, and there's a reason for that: our bodies are made from earth, water, fire, and air. The same substances that create our planet create our bodies, and Spirit lives in all of it.

The earth is your body. Your physical substance. Your muscles. Your connective tissue. Your body fat.

The water is your blood. The rivers of life in your body. Your sweat. Your tears, which are the ocean within you.

The fire is your spirit. Your soul. Your purpose. Your passion.

The air is your breath. Your intellect. Your invisible thoughts.

We have forgotten where we came from, so when we spend time in nature, it reminds us. This is you. This is Spirit. We all have access to this universal, creative energy, until we block it somehow.

Usually we seek it because we want to be more comfortable . . . more peaceful.

What is peace?

I used to think that peace was about serenity and tranquility. Not anymore. Peace is about accepting what is.

When you're at peace, it infuses your anger, grief, envy, and frustration by saying, "I feel you. It's ok. What are you trying to teach me? What don't I see that I need to see?"

Peace doesn't say, "Oh, go away, you bad feelings! I just want to be peaceful!"

I tried that latter approach when I was healing. It didn't work. Denying the pain just creates more pain.

People effortlessly buy into the idea that if they aren't happy, something is wrong.

Finding peace and healing isn't about eliminating all your bad feelings. It's not about making your life perfect or looking perfect.

As I mentioned earlier, healing was a very uncomfortable process for me. Over time, as my head cleared, I figured something out: if you look closely at the wellness movement, you often see fear masked with a glowing smile.

Fear of aging.

Fear of getting sick.

Fear of dying.

Discovering peace and vitality means that you face these fears head on, not ignore them. You celebrate aging because you are still here. You know that illness IS an opportunity for healing. As for dying, you realize that death is part of the sacred cycle of life.

Your vitality is in your hands. There is hope.

In this book, I will teach you about areas in your life where you can build your vitality, and how to know when to step into discomfort instead of away from it.

Obviously, our world is complex. Socioeconomic factors and the stresses they create are real. Systemic oppression of people of color and women, widening economic gaps, and corporate greed are far beyond the scope of this book, but I must acknowledge that these factors contribute to the inability of many people to make positive changes in their lives.

My hope is that there is something for everyone in this book. This book is about taking your power back. It is about the things you can do. You get to choose what is manageable, and each step you take will open you up to the next one.

Once you start using these skills, you will start to see positive changes, which will allow you to build trust, first in yourself and then in the Universe. As you do this work, you will regain your power. You won't need certainty, because you will have faith. You'll have confidence, so you won't have to run to so-called experts because you are scared. If you do turn to an expert, it will be for guidance and advice that you will incorporate into your own research, not because you want someone to give you instructions to blindly follow.

With power comes a surge of energy. With greater energy comes awareness. When awareness and energy align, we tap into our vitality.

When I was lying in a hospital bed years ago, ill, my light was dull. Now, thanks to the skills I learned and will share in this book, my light is brighter.

This divine Spiritual energy, the substance of the oneness that creates everything, wants to move through you in a specific way. I want to show you to how to access this flow.

Instead of forcing an agenda onto your body, this book is about life finding you. The self-help and wellness movements are all about setting goals. "What do you want to achieve in your life? Write it down and do it!"

I lived this way for decades. I created oodles of vision boards with pictures of all the things I wanted to manifest.

I thought my life would be perfect if I had a flat stomach.

I was in control of my destiny!

I was in control of my body!

I prided myself on setting goals and achieving them, but what I didn't realize was that I was ignoring my body. It was yelling at me. It started out softly and then the screaming got louder and louder. This went on for years, until I finally collapsed.

I am here to tell you your body is never wrong. It is your greatest teacher. It is sacred ground.

In his book *Turning Pro*, Stephen Pressfield says, "The physical leads to the spiritual."[1] When you take care of your body in the right way, you step into vitality. And vitality is the source of miracles.

I'm living proof. I once suffered, just like you may be, but the skills I learned and will share with you changed my entire life, as well as my body.

CHAPTER 1

MY STORY

"How do the geese know when to fly to the sun?
Who tells them the seasons?
How do we humans know when it is time to move on?
As with the migrant birds, so surely with us,
there is a voice within, if only we would listen to it,
that tells us so certainly when to go
forth into the unknown."

—ELIZABETH KUBLER-ROSS

This is my story.

I grew up in Richmond, Texas, a small town on the outskirts of Houston. My dad worked up the road in Sugar Land at the Imperial Sugar Company. Over the years he made the best of corporate America and worked his way up to Vice President of Transportation.

All I ever heard growing up in the 1980s was that sugar was good for you. It was natural, only 16 calories per teaspoon, non-fat, and studies showed that it caused no behavioral problems in school-age children.

And yet, my nickname as a kid was The Exorcist.

I earned the nickname because when I got hungry, I acted possessed. At my worst, I had violent temper tantrums that I couldn't control. I once kicked a hole in the wall of my parent's bedroom. I couldn't control myself, unless I had food in my tummy.

You may be familiar with this feeling. Today we often call it "hangry," a cross between hungry and angry. It's caused by a drop in blood-sugar levels. The body is smart. When blood-sugar levels drop, the brain redirects its resources to survival mode. Emotions become primal. It's not a pretty sight. A lot of people, especially kids, exhibit "hangriness." I will take this moment to remind you that just because something is common doesn't mean it's normal, and just because the word "hangry" is funny doesn't mean it's ok.

In middle school, I always struggled in the class before lunch. One day, I was so ravenously hungry that I violently dug my pen back and forth into my paper until it ripped and the pen gouged the desk. The teacher escorted me out of the room and called my parents to talk about my unusual behavior.

Their explanation was the same as always: "Well, that's just the way she is when she's hungry. Not sure what to do."

Meanwhile, I enjoyed sugar at every opportunity, even at breakfast.

Damn, I loved donuts. Every Saturday morning my dad would take me to our local bakery, where I was free to pick out my breakfast. I always ordered the same thing: a glazed donut, a chocolate donut, a cake donut, 6 donut holes, a cream cheese kolache, and either a cupcake or an iced sugar cookie.

When my friends spent the night, they would come along with dad and me and only order one donut. Astonished, I assumed they were just trying to be polite. I would always say, "You can have more!"

I ate dessert after every single meal, and as I grew older, I started to plan my meal around dessert. If I had a heavy meal with something like a steak or enchiladas, then I would have a light dessert, like angel food cake.

If I ate a lighter meal, like fish or chicken, then I would eat a heavier dessert, like cheesecake.

My love for sugar was so intertwined with who I was that my whole life was centered on it. When I fantasized about what I would be when I grew up, I decided that I wanted to do what I loved, which was bake. I had dreams of having a bakery called Room For Dessert. Sugar made me happy—very happy—and I wanted to devote my life to making other people happy, too.

The thing is, I was a happy kid, but I was a sick one, too. No one ever thought to wonder why.

I couldn't breathe!

I lived on steroids, antibiotics, antihistamines, and inhalers as a child. My most vivid childhood memory isn't playing with friends. It's of me lying on the couch, watching cartoons, snuggling in a blanket, with my mom leaning over me asking, "Are the people singing in your chest, sweetie?"

I was diagnosed with severe asthma when I was 3 years old. If you have suffered from this, then you know that wheezing is good. It means there's some air getting into your lungs. No wheezing at all means that you're about to be in serious trouble.

When I was in sixth grade, my parents took me to an allergy specialist who gave me weekly shots, but that only made me worse. A few months into the treatment, I was taking so many allergy medications with stimulating side effects that I ate just enough food to survive.

I had no appetite. I lost 35 pounds in a month.

Up until this point, I hadn't given my physical body much thought. Nobody ever said I was overweight, so I had no reason to think otherwise.

Then, other moms started calling my mom, saying, "Wow. Charlotte looks great. What diet are you using?" Boys started to pay attention to me.

While outsiders were celebrating my appearance, my family was deeply concerned about my well-being.

One day at the doctor's office, my mom looked at me and then looked around the waiting room and thought, "No one here looks healthy. I'm sitting here with a bunch of zombies!" Smart woman. I'm so glad that she saw what she needed to see that day. We left the office and saw my pediatrician, who recommended that we stop all the medications and allergy shots and see if my appetite came back.

Within a few days, I started eating again and my strength returned. What no one knew was that I started counting calories and restricting my food choices in an effort to maintain my new, skinny body. I was 13 years old, which marked the beginning of years of uncontrollable bingeing, deprivation, and excessive exercise.

I know my parents loved me, and the doctors wanted to make me better. Everyone was doing the best they could, but nothing ever worked. Eventually we just surrendered to it. Charlotte wheezes. She turns into The Exorcist sometimes. That's just Charlotte.

Ironically, I became a competitive swimmer. It was almost as if my body wanted to take what was weak and make it strong. I swam throughout college and then participated in triathlons, with my inhaler in my hand. All along, I fueled myself with energy drinks and sugar, calming my nerves in the evening with sweet alcoholic beverages. Everyone thought I was healthy. Heck, I thought I was healthy! I looked fit and ate a low-fat diet and did all the "right" things.

Sweet dreams

After graduating from college, I decided to pursue my dream of owning a bakery. I got a job waiting tables in a restaurant while I sold cakes out of my home. Many times I worked double shifts, staying up late and getting up early. Eventually, I worked my way into a management position. But I was utterly exhausted.

I was so tired I stopped competing in triathlons. My life was whittled down to an endless cycle of working, sleeping, and watching TV. Then one day, something dramatic happened.

I was 26 years old. My boyfriend and I drove to Dallas to catch a baseball game. After checking into a hotel, I lay down on the bed for a rest. I remember everything about the moment. The crunchy feel of the bedspread on my back. The hideous wallpaper with flowers and stripes. I closed my eyes, and suddenly felt something wash over me, from head to toe. It was a deep, deep ache. A heaviness. A flu-like feeling.

I turned to my boyfriend and said, "Geez, I feel like I'm getting sick. Ugh."

From that minute on, I was in a daze. I could barely walk up a flight of stairs. So I did what I had always done—I went to the doctor, who put me on a round of antibiotics.

I finished the round of antibiotics and wasn't any better, so I went back to my doctor, who put me on another round of antibiotics.

I didn't get any better, so I went back to my doctor, who put me on yet another round of antibiotics.

Now, I was on my fourth week of complete and utter misery. I missed way too many days of work. I visited my doctor again and said, "Something isn't right here. Can you please run some blood work?"

The doctor agreed.

At 10:45 that night, my phone rang. I was in bed, too tired to groan. It was the doctor. She said, "Sweetie, you need to go to the emergency room. Your white blood cell count and your liver enzymes are off the chart."

I said, "Well, what do you think it is?"

She said, "You're probably going to lose your gall bladder."

Excuse me? I think I would like to keep my organs!

So I headed to the emergency room. After $5,000 worth of tests, they told me my gall bladder was healthy.

I had been in the ER all night, scared and helpless, wondering how in the world I'd gotten there. I had taken a nutrition class in college. I was an athlete. I was pursuing my dreams of a bakery.

It never occurred to me that I had been sick for a long, long time. Asthma and wildly fluctuating blood sugar levels were so much a part of me that I didn't even think about it.

Mysteries solved, sort of

My world turned upside down that night. As I lay there with an IV in my arm, wondering what was going to become of me, I knew deep down that I was responsible for this situation. Being a victim was not an option. I made a vow to myself: "Charlotte, when you get out of here, and you will, you are going to find a career that involves health. Real health. Something where you have to be well in order to do the work."

A while later, I heard doctors talking outside my room. A new shift had shown up, and one of them said, "Has anyone tested her for mono? She's a textbook case."

The $15 mono spot test came back positive.

They told me to go home, drink lots of water, and rest.

That advice wouldn't be enough. I didn't know it at the time, but my life as I knew it was completely over. In general, the younger you are when you get mononucleosis, the milder it is and the quicker the recovery, but at age 26, I was hit hard, and it was years before I felt well.

I didn't have the energy to do much of anything. However, my boyfriend at the time was moving to California to pursue his master's degree. I clearly needed a change of scene, so I went with him. Things didn't get any better in California. I took 3-hour naps during the day and slept 12 hours each night, and I still felt tired.

Then, things got even worse. I passed out five times in restaurants. I would be hungry and order my food, then start to feel funny. My lips would turn blue and before the food arrived, BAM! I'd be on the floor. The paramedics would show up, asking all their worst-case scenario questions: "Ma'am, do you do drugs? Is there any chance that you could be pregnant?"

"No," I would reply with a sigh. "Nothing that exciting. I just didn't eat soon enough."

Two very extraordinary things happened next. The first

was when I called my insurance company to find a local doctor. I needed to get blood work to make sure my liver enzymes and white blood cells came back into normal range. They put me in touch with a holistic doctor. Who would have believed it?

This woman was wonderful. She listened to me and, based on my history and fainting episodes, recommended that I go for a blood glucose tolerance test. It came back positive for reactive hypoglycemia, a condition in which your body is unable to regulate blood sugar, leaving you without enough for your brain to use as fuel. This causes shakiness, headaches, and other unpleasant symptoms. I was fainting because as soon as my body used up the sugar from my last meal, my blood sugar levels would crater.

Well, that was one mystery solved. My new doctor referred me to a nutritionist down the road, who had a 6-week waiting list.

While I was waiting for my appointment, the second extraordinary thing happened.

My boyfriend said, "You should talk to my friend. He had something similar happen and he read a book about it that helped. Here's his number. Call him."

I called his friend, who did indeed have a story very similar to mine, and discovered that the only way he could heal was to give up sugar. He told me to read a book by Dr. Robert Atkins, a pioneer in the low-carbohydrate movement.

While I was removing refined carbohydrates like sugar from my diet, I had my appointment with the nutritionist, who was very helpful with specific supplements and dietary advice. I still wanted more information, however, so I asked her, "Where did you study this?"

She said, "At a school up the road in Santa Cruz. It's called the Institute for Educational Therapy." (Now it's called Bauman College.)

So I started their two-year Nutrition Consultant program, and began learning how to eat. My body had a lot of things to work out. I suffered from:

> Severe headaches
>
> Embarrassing hot flashes (out of nowhere my face would turn beet red)
>
> 6 months of diarrhea
>
> Gas and bloating
>
> Fatigue, fatigue, and more fatigue
>
> Overall body aches
>
> Mental fog
>
> Allergic attacks with sneezing and asthma
>
> Incessant nasal drip
>
> Frequent infections of all sorts
>
> Burning stomach
>
> Emotional roller coasters with unpredictable fits of crying and anger
>
> Chemical sensitivities

Profuse sweating

Debilitating depression and anxiety

After years of being in control of my body, it was now in control of me.

Every time I went to friend's home or spent the night in a hotel, I suffered from an allergic attack. My eyes would water. My nose would run. My face would turn bright red. I was miserable. I felt like my world was shrinking. Changing environments made my body so sick. I would finally plan something fun, show up, and then just want to leave.

I detested not being able to keep commitments. I would make plans with a new friend, but I just couldn't follow through with any activity that wasn't 100% necessary. All my energy went to school, my part-time job, and my close relationships. I felt profoundly isolated when what I needed more than anything was connection.

Between recovering from the mononucleosis infection and giving up sugar, there was nothing left for me to give at the end of the day.

Most people just don't understand how hard it can be to give up sugar. It is much like going through substance withdrawal, but unlike alcoholics or drug addicts, you have nowhere to go for support. Where is the support group or recovery house for a body learning how to be in the world without refined carbohydrates?

These were very, very dark times. The hardest part of

it all was that I looked fine, even healthy. Nobody had any idea how horrible I felt.

My ability to handle stress was very low. The tiniest thing could put me over the edge. One day I had an appointment, but when I got into my car, I realized that I didn't have any gas. I couldn't deal with it. I started crying and ended up canceling my appointment.

Most people would have just driven to the gas station, right? Seems simple enough, but not when chronic inflammation distorts your thinking, and logic goes out the window.

I constantly berated myself for my inability to cope with life.

It was like my spirit was trapped in a somewhat lifeless body.

My boyfriend thought I was depressed, and recommended that I see a therapist. After a few sessions, I realized that I couldn't think my way out of this illness. It was in my body. But I did get something great from this therapist. She pointed me to Elaine Aron's book, *The Highly Sensitive Person: How to Thrive When the World Overwhelms You.* It was helpful. I didn't feel so alone any more. This book taught me that some people's nervous systems are just wired differently and may need more care.

An essential aspect of my healing was accepting that after all these years of trying to prove myself and control my body, the tables I had turned. I had no choice now but to surrender to my body.

Eventually, I graduated from my nutrition program,

and we moved to the Washington, DC area for my boy-friend's new job.

I took a job with a fair amount of flexibility at a sports club, in sales. I was sick every month with an infection that corresponded to my menstrual cycle. I had an asymptomatic bladder infection, along with chronic bacterial vaginosis. I was somehow able to keep my job, but I slept a lot.

One day, a friend begged me to go to an herbal fair with her. I was so unenthusiastic, I went in my pajamas. Once there, however, I had a good time, especially after I came upon a purple table hosted by two wonderful women representing the Tai Sophia Institute (now the Maryland University of Integrative Health). I had wanted more education, and realized after talking with them that herbal medicine would be the perfect companion to nutrition. It was just one of those moments of deep knowing that this was what I needed to do. Shortly thereafter, I left my job to begin a three-year masters of science degree in Western herbal medicine.

By this point, you're probably wondering, "You say that you were sick, but how does a sick person move to California, complete a two-year nutrition program while holding down a part-time job, and then move to DC and take on a three-year master's program?"

I have a three-part answer to that question. One, my loved ones helped me financially. Two, I wanted to learn about what had happened to me. I wanted to answer the questions: How did I become so miserable, and how can I feel alive again? Three, I didn't know it at the time, but a larger hand was moving me through all the discomforts. Spirit was with me.

Healing requires action, even when you are sick. No matter how bad I felt, I just knew that I had to do something.

With my decision to start school, I was feeling hopeful about the future. All the hard work of changing my diet and lifestyle habits seemed to be paying off. I had bad days and bad weeks, but there were some good ones as well.

Then, I started to have a lot of bad days.

Man's best friend was my worst nightmare

We bought a dog. A cute little white West Highland Terrier named Fonzie. Within days, my asthma flared up. I had a severe allergy to Fonzie. I was depressed, with unimaginable fatigue. My body ached all over. The headaches returned. It would take me 30 minutes to write a three-sentence e-mail. Despite all my dietary changes, I wanted to sleep all the time. It felt like I was back at square one.

I did my best to show up in life and act normal, but that was even more exhausting.

One morning, I found myself barely able to walk to the bathroom. My legs were so heavy that I shuffled to go pee. I was 30 years old and could barely walk across the room. In the bathroom mirror I saw a red rash around my hairline. I leaned up against the wall, slid down to the floor, and cried. I cried until I couldn't cry anymore.

Why was this happening? How much longer would this go on? I didn't want to live like this. I didn't have a plan for suicide but I thought about it. Please, please, I mentally called out to Spirit. Please. Help me.

As I sat there on the floor, in complete and utter despair, I realized I must still be here for a reason.

Standing up

Winston Churchill said, "If you are going through Hell, keep going."

Suddenly, my despair turned into anger. Life has too much value for me to be a useless puddle of mush.

Three simple words got me off the bathroom floor: Fuck. This. Shit.

So I did what people do. I stood up, brushed my teeth, and I took care of all the day-to-day business that is easy for most people, but was really hard for me.

A few days went by, and I was back at school. A graduate of my program came to talk about life as a clinician. I liked his vibe and thought maybe he could help me, so I made an appointment with him.

During my consultation, I told him everything: how much my body hurt, how desperate I was feeling, how I felt that no one was really listening to me. He listened patiently, asked a lot of questions, and then sent me home with a customized liquid herbal formula.

I took one dose in my car that afternoon and then another one before I went to bed.

My transformation

The next morning, I woke up, sat on the edge of my bed, and realized that my body felt different. I felt relaxed, like my shoulders had dropped from my ears, and I felt more fluid in my movement. When I walked across the room to go to the bathroom, my feet came up off the floor. Effortlessly.

I was the same, but I was very, very different. Not only was my body relaxed, but so was my mind. I never realized how much brain fog I had until it was gone. The incessant mental chatter was replaced with a stillness that I had never experienced.

For the first time in my life, I felt normal. Now, I know that normal is a loaded word, but up until this point, I had never had that "I'm ok, you're ok" feeling.

I felt the presence of Spirit everywhere.

I went to the kitchen, ate breakfast, and then headed to a Laundromat. I sang to the music in my car. When was the last time I had sung? When I got to the Laundromat, I actually wanted to be there. I was happy to be there, folding my clothes. I wasn't thinking about the conversation I had had earlier with my boyfriend. I wasn't thinking about how unprepared I was for an upcoming test, or about that project that I needed to finish.

I just folded my laundry.

I felt present in my life, and it was beautiful.

Later, my friends and classmates could see something was different about me. It wasn't just that I was wearing a little make-up and clothes that made me feel good. They told me I was glowing.

I felt filled with light. It was like an exorcism had actually occurred overnight. Taking my herbal formula facilitated a spiritual experience of touching something that altered my life forever.

More changes

A few weeks later, I made some more big changes. After hearing about my frequent, urgent bowel movements, my herbalist recommended that I remove gluten from my diet. Going gluten-free was effortless, and relieved a significant amount of inflammation in my body. My digestion improved. After a session with my massage therapist, I didn't hurt all over. She even commented, "Your tissue feels different."

After a few more weeks, I ended things with my boyfriend. There was no way we could recover from the damage that my chronic inflammation had done to our relationship. We weren't supposed to be together any more.

(In case you were wondering, he got the dog.)

I rented a sweet little basement apartment and enjoyed my clinical training and the hope of a new life. I still had a few bad days here and there, but nothing like before. I just focused on taking good care of myself, sleeping eight to nine hours each night, and eating good food.

I finally started to meditate. And I made an effort to get closer to nature. Every day I went on a walk. At the end of it, I would take my shoes off and cool my feet in a beautiful stream near my apartment. I'd just sit there and repeat a simple prayer of thank you. Over and over again. Thank you. It felt so good.

But not *everything* felt good. Graduation from school was bittersweet. I missed my classmates. I had two job opportunities that should have worked out, but didn't. Ending my long-term relationship had set me free, but I felt ungrounded. I started to question if this was where I needed to be living. Did I want to build a life in McLean, Virginia? If I didn't, it was time to make a move, and sooner rather than later. Shortly after this realization, something happened.

The voice

One night I found myself sitting up in bed. I heard a voice that seemed inside my head, but outside of me. It said, "You could move home to Texas."

There was something much bigger than me in my bedroom that night, but it wasn't scary. It was kind and direct. It was Spirit.

I looked at the clock. It was 3 a.m. I rolled over and went back to sleep.

The next day, I called home to talk to my parents about moving back to Texas. My parents were living in the Hill Country outside Austin. Austin sounded like a good idea. Within 48 hours, I was making plans.

I landed in Austin in October of 2008 and continued to work on the idea of my Eat in Peace Wellness Consulting business. Not long after, I attended a nutrition and herbal seminar where the course of my life was altered—again.

Love at last

As I sat in the seminar, the teacher made a comment that made the hair on my neck stand up. My body was covered in goose bumps. He said, "Spirit enters the body through the HPA axis."

The herbal formula that had resulted in a profound spiritual experience for me was geared towards what's called the hypothalamic-pituitary-adrenal (HPA) axis. This is the stress response—what gets you out of bed in the morning and saves you when you almost get in a wreck.

Now, things were starting to make sense! But who could tell me more? One meant-to-be conversation after another directed me to the man who would become my husband: Glenn.

Glenn is the sales representative for the line of supplements I use, called Standard Process and MediHerb. He hosted the seminar where I learned that Spirit enters the body through the HPA axis. We had lunch on December 2nd, 2008, and were pretty much inseparable from that point on.

We started to build a life together.

I maintained my business and started to work in his as well. As time went on, I realized I couldn't keep up, so I sent a prayer out every day: "Infinite Spirit, show me the way. My life is not sustainable. What do I do? Do I give more to Glenn's business or put more energy in mine? Show me."

Six months went by. I was getting antsy.

Then, we got a big surprise. I found out I was pregnant! Motherhood was my next step. Who knew?

Despite my once very ill body, I experienced an amazing pregnancy and gave birth to our son at the foot of our bed. I should point out that in the months after his birth, the medical system surely would have diagnosed me with post-partum depression. I was in a sleep-deprived stupor. Every day was the same. What just happened to my life? I had figured everything out. I knew how to care for myself, but not another human being!

However, I knew deep in my bones that much more was going on than "depression." I had been here before, during my healing process. I was in a period of deep transformation—again! Without this dark experience of motherhood, I'm certain that you would not have this book in your hands. Giving up my previous life opened me up to an entirely new one.

Not only am I now a mother, but after thirty years with asthma, I can breathe without drugs. Along the way, I discovered that I never really had asthma; I had a dairy sensitivity.

Vitality isn't something that just happened to me. It is something that I co-create every day. I listen to my body, and I listen to what life is trying to tell me.

My life is not shits and giggles and unicorn farts.

I am doing the work. All. The. Time.

When I hurt, I don't try to escape it. Instead, I inquire into it. To me, a life of vitality is a repeating pattern of dying and being reborn—going deep into the winter to enjoy the spring. I fall into the darkness and I reach for the light.

I want you to achieve the same freedom and confidence and ease of movement. Through learning to trust your body, you CAN learn to trust all of life.

I am going to teach you what I've learned. All the accumulated knowledge from my formal education, clinical observations, and personal study and experience is here for you in this handbook.

The first thing I did was to change my relationship to food. So let's start there.

CHAPTER 2

EAT IN PEACE

Musician Warren Zevon appeared on David Letterman's
show after he discovered he had cancer.
Letterman asked him, "From your perspective,
do you know something about life . . . that maybe
I don't know?"
Zevon replied, "I know how much you're supposed to
enjoy every sandwich."[2]

The origins of Eating in Peace

When I was growing up, the phone number to our house was 342-8878. Sonic's, the fast food restaurant, was 342-8788. Almost every night at dinnertime, the phone would ring with calls for Sonic. If my father had imbibed enough cocktails, he might take the caller's to-go order. As a child, I thought this was hilarious. Meanwhile, my mom would throw her hands up in the air, exasperated, and say, "Dammit! Why does that phone always ring when we sit down to dinner? Why can't we just eat in peace?"

Decades later, when I was in school studying nutrition, I put together a presentation for my final class project about blood sugar regulation. As I was drawing on a white easel (this was way before Power Point presentation), I saw that my dinner plate showing how to create a meal looked like a peace sign.

So there it was. Eat in Peace found me in childhood and manifested years later as my life's work.

The power of food

Food literally creates us. Have you ever noticed that the word EAT is in create? I have. I do not think that is a coincidence.

More and more people are using their resources and asking the right questions to find a lifestyle that helps them feel their best. They are even healing themselves of diseases, like diabetes, autoimmune disorders, and cancer, which continue to stupefy the medical system. What most of them discover is that the #1 culprit for their former misery was the food they ate.

These are the lucky ones, but too many people are still in the dark about how food affects our bodies and our minds. It's no coincidence that as our lives have gotten busier and we've started prioritizing convenience over nutrition, many people have reported feeling that their health has declined.

Food is either nourishing your body or destroying it.

I learned the 13 principles of eating in peace as I overcame my own struggle with food, whether it was my sugar addiction or my food sensitivities. I lost control of what I was consuming. Instead of nourishing me, food was consuming me, and it was destroying my life.

It's really, really hard to address food cravings on your own or change your eating habits without guidance and structure. But in this chapter, instead of telling you specifically what to eat, I'm going to give you guidelines on how to *think* about food so you can recognize which ones make you feel good, and which ones don't. I want your food choices to be self-directed, not imposed upon you by me, the media, or any other expert. No one is a better expert on your body than you, and you'll be more likely to stick to your good decisions when they come from within.

Learning to eat this way is what helped me heal. It was a slow process, but it is based in wisdom and truth. It is real, like the food you should be eating.

1. Eat real food.

Eating well is simple: If you could not find it 10,000 years ago, then it is probably not food.

Here are some specific guidelines for you:

- If you cannot pick it, grow it, fish it, raise it, or hunt it, then it is also probably not food.

- Talk to your food. Ask it where it came from. Did you come from a tree or the sea? Or a bush? Were you living on a farm? Or flying in the sky? This is a great game to play with kids.

- Eat foods that spoil (but before they do).

- Do not worry about overeating. As your body adapts to eating real food, your unique physiology will determine the best proportions and types of meats, fats, vegetables, fruits, dairy, grains, legumes, nuts, and seeds to eat. Yes, there may be times when you binge (if that is your tendency), but any set-back is just another opportunity for forward movement. You learn something and you recommit yourself to your healing path.

- Say goodbye to meal plans and diets that claim their methods are foolproof and universal. Experts can offer you experiments, not answers. It is up to you to find your inner power and decide what does and doesn't work for you.

- Stick close to nature. As philosopher Alan Watts said: "You didn't come into this world. You came out of it, like a wave from the ocean. You are not a stranger here."

Yet we are so disconnected from this world! I have met very intelligent people who, when I recommend that they stop consuming dairy, exclaimed, "You mean I can't have eggs?"

Huh? Eggs are NOT dairy! The only thing milk and eggs have in common is that they are both white and sold in the refrigerated section of the supermarket.

When you eat real food, you are connecting to the very beginning of Life. All the wisdom of humanity passes down to you through food. When you look at the sky to marvel over a sunrise or a sunset, gaze at the stars, or watch clouds passing by, remember that our ancestors did the same thing. They looked at the same sky, bathed in the same water, cooked with the same fire. That's why nature soothes the nervous system. It reconnects us to our origins. Real food does the same thing.

There is an adage in interior design: bring the outside in. We need to do the same for our bodies. Most people know in their bones that spending time in nature is good for us (if you need the science behind this, check out the work of Richard Louv and look into forest bathing). They just find it difficult to get outside.

I would argue that eating real food is even more important than spending time in nature, because the inside of your digestive tract has the surface area of a studio apartment.

What you put into your body matters. So many people

want a clear-cut plan for what to eat. Unfortunately, that just does not exist. Eating, like life, isn't just an intellectual exercise in decision-making. It is visceral.

Aside from the general advice of eating food found in nature, no one can tell you which specific foods are good for you. Your nutritional needs will shift over time. Occasionally, it will be crystal clear which foods you should eat or avoid. More often than not, you will be in the unknown. But trust your body, and the fear of the unknown will morph into faith, not only when you eat, but in all aspects of your life.

The idea that your external environment is different from what is going on inside your body is an illusion. You are a part of the whole. The matrix present in real food hooks you into the flow of the entire universe. Processed foods, synthetic vitamins, and pharmaceutical drugs simply cannot do that.

That said, sometimes real food isn't enough to heal you, particularly in the face of chronic disease. At some point, your body may ask you to take on a more extreme diet. You may find that you need to eliminate (either temporarily or long-term) entire food groups, like grains and diary, from your diet, which brings me to my next point.

2. Accept that food is controversial, and that in the end, all you can do is trust yourself.

Experts scream, "Look, over here, I've got THE best diet ever!" On one hand you have fruitarians promoting raw foods, and on the other, proponents of the ketogenic diet tell you to eat fat all day long. And then there's the faction that keeps crooning, "everything in moderation."

My personal favorite: "The Blood Type Diet changed my life!"

Really? Did it? Because I don't think that's what changed your life. It's just a theory that will never be proven, not to mention that indigenous people had all the blood types. Then there's the impracticality of it all. How does a mother feed her family when each family member has a different blood type? Please, let's not make eating harder than it needs to be.

Are these people or any specific diet wrong? No.

Are they right? No.

Diets and meal plans are appealing because they give you directions to follow without having to think too much for yourself, but you should be wary of anything that fits into a neat box. People and life just aren't like that! Certainty is an illusion. Many diets work because they provide a structure and largely remove processed, inflammatory foods from our diets, but they are rarely, if ever, a long-term solution.

If you follow a specific diet, look at it as an experiment—an opportunity to learn something about yourself and food.

Bottom line: food falls into the same category as sex, money, politics, religion, and parenting. It is controversial, emotional, and personal, and it brings up a lot of ideals and attachments.

It has the capacity to bring us together or drive us apart.

One time, my husband and I picked up a chiropractor at the airport. She specializes in nutrition and was to speak at our conference center the next day. Somehow, during the ride to the hotel, we started talking about breakfast.

I said, "We have a joke in our house. When we wake up in the morning, my husband says, 'Hey, sweetie. Do you want eggs and bacon? Or bacon and eggs?"

She chuckled and said, "Wow. You guys must really love parasites."

I wanted to reach over into the backseat and strangle her.

"No, I don't love parasites. I LOVE PORK!" I wanted to scream. Somehow, I managed to keep my mouth shut and smile.

One person's poison is another person's medicine.

Expect issues to come up around food, and when they do, you won't be surprised. Food is as complex as you are.

3. Enjoy whatever you eat.

Most of us have had this thought run through our head at mealtimes: "I should eat this, it is good for me, but instead, I am going to eat that, which is bad for me. I deserve it. I had a rough day."

All food has a purpose. Some food is just fun. Other foods are just healthy. We want both. We want food to be fun *and* healthy,

But there's something else here that I want to talk to you about.

Food is not a reward system. It is the substance of life.

Sometimes life sucks. Being human is hard. The modern world is challenging. Don't mask those very real moments of frustration and anxiety with food.

Sure, we will comfort ourselves with food from time to time, and that's ok. Just remember that there are so many other ways to reward yourself, instead of pleasure at the expense of health. You can take a bath or extra long shower, have a special cup of tea with a friend, or go to a movie. It does not have to be a pint of ice cream. But when it is, enjoy every freaking bite.

"Should" creates tension and promotes feelings of guilt. Guilt and shame will never bring you peace. According to traditional Chinese medicine, guilt is the main emotion responsible for halting the flow of chi in the body. Chi is just another word for life-giving energy, which creates vitality.

If you are going to fully enjoy what you eat, then you must let go of the guilt and be fully present to the experience of eating, especially when it's a food whose sole purpose is your pleasure.

Then you may realize that it doesn't make you feel so good after all.

Like many, you might think that "healthy eating" is just code for deprivation. You are mistaken. As I stated earlier, Eating in Peace involves choosing foods that you can enjoy AND that nourish your body, but that doesn't exclude an occasional indulgence. Just make sure it's worth it! This is especially important early on in your healing process as you let go of foods that do not create vitality.

4. How matters more than what.

How you eat is more important than *what* you eat because *how* you eat will change *what* you eat.

As I said earlier, the reason so many diets don't work is that they impose a specific structure of eating on your life, as opposed to allowing you to make food choices that come from deep knowledge that this is what's good for you.

There was a story that floated around the school where I studied herbal medicine. An acupuncturist in student clinic had a client with back pain. As he did his extensive intake at their first consultation, he realized that his client's diet was dramatically contributing to his inflammation. This man was like something out of that documentary, *Super Size Me*, where director Morgan Spurlock eats every meal at a fast-food restaurant. He drove a lot for his job and ate in his car all day long, hopping from one fast-food restaurant to the next.

After the acupuncturist expressed concern, his client said, "Look, I just want you to help me with the pain in my back, ok? I don't want to change my diet."

So the acupuncturist did just that. When they were saying goodbye, the acupuncturist said, "I know you're not interested in changing your diet, but since I helped you with your back and I will be seeing you next week, can you do one thing for me?"

The client shrugged, as if to say maybe.

"When you eat, go into the restaurant, sit down, and enjoy your meal. Keep eating what you're eating. Just don't do it in your car. How does that sound?" The client agreed.

When he came in for his next appointment, the client said, "So I did what you told me to do. I went into the restaurant and ate. I didn't like the smell. And the food didn't even taste that good. I'm in such a hurry during the day, I just wasn't paying any attention. So yes, ok, maybe I could use some dietary advice."

Isn't that story rich?

The fast-paced nature of our modern world tells us there are more important things to do than eat. Almost every day I see a new advertisement somewhere for a meal replacement shake or bar that will solve all of your problems. They promise weight loss, increased energy and nutrition, and convenience. They promote themselves as life-savers because they require less time to eat so you can work more.

Life-savers my butt. As Royal Lee, founder of the nutrition company Standard Process and one of the great thinkers of our time, said, "We are digging our graves with our teeth."

Buyer beware: man-made food products can never replace food. Food is more than the sum of its parts.

We can no longer afford to let our busy-ness interrupt the very important rituals of meals. People's bodies and even their families are falling apart because we have our priorities all backwards. Granted, it's not all our fault. We have major problems in our corporate structures that ask for more and more from their employees. The solution to that problem is beyond the scope of this book. However, one thing that can possibly change is YOU. It is up to YOU to restore and create the sacred space associated with eating.

Taking time to eat real meals is about taking control of your life. When it feels like a thousand things are trying to get your attention, you can reclaim your life by choosing to eat in peace. In taking this simple action, you are bringing sanity to yourself, your family, your community, and the world. Sitting down to eat consciously is a quiet act of resistance in a world that doesn't ever want to stop. Eating is a way to rest and retreat during a busy day. In essence, you are changing the world by making the decision to sit down, eat, and enjoy your meal.

Doesn't that make you feel powerful?

I sure hope so.

I was scrolling through my Instagram feed the other day. One of the authors I follow had a picture of her breakfast next to her computer. She is writing a new cookbook. Underneath the picture, she said something to the effect of, "It's a working breakfast this morning! I've got a deadline for my new book. No time to spare!"

Most people would celebrate her commitment and discipline. There was a time when I would have admired her. "Look at that. How inspiring. A woman after her own dreams."

This time I thought, however, "How disappointing. She thinks that what she's *doing* is more important than *being* with her body and food. It only takes about 10 minutes to sit down and eat a meal in peace. She went to all that trouble to prepare a beautiful breakfast and now she won't fully enjoy it."

Bottom line: when you eat, EAT!

Here are some simple yet specific suggestions that may help you.

- Sit down.
- Set your table (yes, even if you are eating alone).
- Light a candle.
- Weather permitting, eat outside.
- If possible, put your utensils aside and eat with your hands. Feel your food.
- Focus on your meal.
- Enjoy it.
- Savor it.
- Feel it in your mouth.
- Feel it in your body.
- Fall in love with your food.
- Fall in love with yourself.
- Fall in love with your family. Yes, this means looking each other in the eyes and having conversations with your loved ones. Turn off the cell phones, the television, and the computers. Texting is *not* talking. Families that eat together, stay together.
- Do NOT eat standing up.
- Do NOT eat at your desk.
- Do NOT eat with technology. Turn off your TV. Put

your phone and your computer away (yes, pleasant music and company are allowed).

- Do NOT read while you eat.
- Do NOT eat in your car.
- Do NOT eat in a highly emotional state.

Notice how difficult it is to do these things—and for some people, it may be nearly impossible, due to trauma around food. If this is your situation or if you suffer from an eating disorder, please get professional help. I recently completed an online program called "Feast: Becoming a Well-Fed Woman," created by Rachel Cole, that would be very appropriate for any woman wanting to be more comfortable in her body and with food.

For me, eating has become a form of meditation. Some people sit still on a cushion and say "Ooooommmmm." Me? At least three times per day, I sit down, check in with my body, and enjoy the hell out of a good meal. Yuuuummmmmm.

If I don't, I suffer. My suffering may not be immediate, but it will visit me later in a lack of energy or mental clarity. I will be less vital for it.

Enjoying food is a gateway into the spiritual realm and truly enjoying life. Nothing is selfish about that. That is living. That is presence. Try to eat each meal as if it could be your last.

After all, food is the very thing that gives us life.

5. Eating is intimate.

Making love and eating have a lot in common.

They are both sensual activities. When you are fully present to a good meal or you are loving your partner, all of your senses are engaged. Through your senses you are literally taking the person, or the food, into your body, mind, and soul. You are in a heightened state of awareness.

You touch.

You smell.

You see.

You hear.

You taste.

Lovemaking is an intimate activity, a sacred union between two people. There is you, your partner, and the energy that you make together. It is act of creation.

So it is with eating.

Eating is an intimate activity, a sacred union between you and food. What you eat becomes you. It is an act of creating the energy that your body, your thoughts, and your emotions need to fully function.

There is no such thing as casual lovemaking and no such thing as casual eating.

Think about it: what could be more disappointing than lovemaking minus the love?

Eating empty calories when your body is expecting real food? That comes close.

Lovemaking without love and eating without nourishment deplete your life force, and will never satisfy your soul's deep yearning to connect.

While you may not make love three times a day on a regular basis, you will eat that often, and maybe more. Make the most of it! Eating is a sacred, repetitive cycle.

Each time you eat, you are reborn.

Each time we eat we make love to ourselves.

It is so beautiful.

Be discerning about who and what you allow into your body. It means something.

6. Food is a metaphor for life.

I said this before, and it's worth repeating: there is no good or bad food. Like all of life, food just IS. We must find a way to relieve the shame around eating so that we can be empowered and free around food. All food has a purpose. Your goal is to make sure the food you eat will promote your health.

Case in point: once I decided to overhaul my diet in 2002, the first thing I did was eliminate white sugar, white flour, white rice, potatoes, and alcohol. I'm not exaggerating—once I had cleaned out my kitchen, I had nothing to eat. So I sat on the kitchen floor, had a good cry, and headed out for a walk.

I kept asking myself:

How can I live without sugar?

What would my family think, given that we had my dad's job at the sugar company to thank for, well, everything?

How would I earn a living if I let go of my career in the food industry?

What would I do with my friends? No more treats?

That's when something profound happened. I remember the cracks on the sidewalk, the beautiful day, the clear air, the blue sky, the sun, and the breeze. A voice in my head answered my questions. It was a voice that both came from deep inside me and yet, was talking to me from outside myself. A voice that I can only identify as Spirit said to me:

"Those foods that you are longing for will always be there. Right now, you need to eat real food—foods that both nourish you and are enjoyable. You can always pick up where you left off. It's your choice. Sugar isn't going anywhere."

I felt my body relax. In that moment, truth found me. Like all of life, food just IS. Sometimes the bad thing that happens to us is really a good thing in disguise. Sugar had brought me joy, connection to others, AND the awareness I needed to change my life.

In that single moment, I could see the Divine Design. Everything was working in my favor.

The whole point was to be able to freely choose what I wanted to put into my body.

I thought, ok, I can do this. I'll be like the alcoholic who continues to attend parties where alcohol is served, but doesn't partake. Alcohol is not inherently bad, and neither is cake. In our culture, cake marks all celebrations—birthday parties, weddings, graduations, potlucks, and holidays.

But while many people can have a slice of cake and carry on with their lives, I cannot.

Sugar was destroying my life, just like alcohol does to an alcoholic. But healing is possible for alcoholics and sugar addicts. Eating well becomes an upward spiral, where each good decision leads to another good decision. And as the minutes, hours, days, months, years, and decades pass by living this way, I realized that life was living me.

Eat well and your vitality emerges. Blessings will find you.

As good food creates you, it's like something inside you longs to create. The reason you are here on this Earth will show itself.

All this, because you decide to align yourself with Spirit, slowing down enough to eat and enjoy food that comes from Mother Nature.

7. Changing the way you eat will change the way you live.

Nothing exists in isolation. As you become more aware of your body and what you put into it, every aspect of your life will shift in a more meaningful way. Eating in peace is an opening to another way of being in the world. Changing the way you eat is a powerful intervention because everyone eats many times a day. If you inventory your eating habits, you'll discover that how you eat mirrors the rest of your life.

Are you enjoying your meals, or rushing through them

to get to your next task? Do you eat in your car? While standing up? Do you skip meals?

Do you take time to prepare a meal at least a few times each week?

It wasn't until I started to really pay attention to food and how it made me feel that I started to wake up to my life. I now had to learn how to cook meals instead of desserts, and I realized that how you do one thing reflects how you do everything.

When you are careless about one aspect of your life, it's likely you are careless about other aspects, too. Every act forges a link, either in your chain of regret or your chain of respect. You are making the choice.

Eating well can be the first step you take to changing the way you live.

Once you begin to eat with intention, you will begin to live with intention, and then, my friend, you will be in a position of great power. You will have a deep inner knowledge of your truth, independent of what is outside of you.

8. Your body doesn't care about your ethics or your morals.

There is one thing that I want to make very clear. In my clinical and personal experience, as well as over a decade of study, you will need to consume some form of animal protein and fat to claim your vitality.

Enjoying bacon isn't a sin. It's healing.

Just as there is no such thing as a good food or a bad

food, what you eat does not make you a good person or a bad person.

Vegan and vegetarian diets are somehow considered holier or purer than those that include animal protein. We need to question this perception. Eating the meat from a cow that ate green grass is just as spiritual as eating kale. And as for people who claim the Bible says not to eat meat: I think God wants us to feel alive and be well, and for many, many people that includes eating animal foods.

That said, I salute vegans and vegetarians for their sensitivity to life and their resistance to the destructive practices of confined animal farming operations. It's just that this way of eating is not a long-term solution for your personal health or the health of the planet. The Savory Institute, for example, is doing a fantastic job of teaching farmers how to use animals to restore the land and topsoil. I also appreciate the work of Diana Rodgers, RD of Sustainable Dish to bring awareness to this topic. She's creating a film titled *Kale Vs. Cow: The Case for Better Meat* (love that title, by the way).

Eating is both an intuitive and intellectual process, and we can both have compassion for animals AND eat animals at the same time. These things are not mutually exclusive.

Many people fail to realize that they come to a vegetarian or vegan lifestyle because of poor digestive capacity. They will say things like, "Over the years, I lost my taste for red meat. Then, I just figured it's not good for you anyway. And I don't like the idea of eating animals, so I will eat a chicken breast or fish sometimes, but not often."

The notion of a healthy or unhealthy food resides solely in the intellect; choosing healthy foods is about listening to your body. If you crave a steak, but you don't eat it because you *think* a vegetarian lifestyle is healthy, you're likely to have a nutritional deficiency. Your body is asking for nourishment, and if you ignore what it wants, you will frequently overeat the wrong foods.

The same phenomenon can manifest with people who think that saturated fats, or fats in general, are problematic, when nothing could be farther from the truth. You might ask yourself, "Why can't I put down that pint of ice cream? Why can't I eat just one potato chip? What's wrong with me?" Nothing is wrong with you. Your body is looking for something it's not getting.

You can eat and still be starving.

For a long time we've been bombarded with the idea that red meat is inherently bad for us. It's absolutely not. Beef builds your blood and muscles and gives you the spirit of a warrior, and in my humble opinion, the world needs people with that kind of spunk. You know, the good spunk—the kind of vitality that comes from enjoying meat. Is beef the ideal protein choice for everyone? Of course not. But it is for some of us. For years I limited this form of protein because the media told me it wasn't a healthy choice. I was ignoring the wisdom of my body, and it loves a good steak! Red meat satiates me and makes me feel strong. Listen to your body. Different meats have different energies and nutritional qualities, and your body can't get everything it needs from a dried up, skinless, boneless chicken breast, and it sure as hell isn't going to get everything it needs from salad greens!

We know that we need to eat a rainbow of vegetables.

We also need to eat a rainbow of meats.

My invitation to you: if red meat or pork or lamb or liver sounds good to you, eat it. Your body is smarter than you think. Don't miss out on animal protein or any other real food because your head gets in the way.

And if animal foods don't sound good to you, then please begin to read and educate yourself about the nutritional value and positive environmental impact of animal foods. Exposing yourself to positive images on social media of eating meat and animal fat can help. Visiting farms that respect the life of animals is healing on many levels as well.

Our misunderstandings on this topic run deep.

I have seen vegan environmentalists at conferences eating processed foods in lieu of animal protein. From my perspective, that is completely lacking in integrity. First, saving the lives of animals while you self-destruct from nutritional deficiencies doesn't do the world any favors. We are the stewards of this earth. Second, avoiding meat will never solve the problems of confined animal farming operations.

The cycle of life and death is inherent in all of nature. Our goal shouldn't be to remove ourselves from that cycle (we can't) but instead to participate in it consciously. There are farms that respect the lives of the animals we eat. Start there.

The one exception to this principle of eating in peace

is if you are following the dietary dictates of your religious beliefs. If so, and you are going to remove a category of food from your diet, please study the resulting nutritional impact on your body, aging, reproductive capacity, and overall vitality. Take the steps necessary to address the deficiency. Consult with a nutritionist or other specialist with experience in this particular area.

9. What you don't eat matters more than what you do eat.

People will praise the latest dietary fad, exclaiming, "This low-fat/low-sugar/low-carbohydrate/all-meat/vegetarian/all-liquid diet changed my life! You've got to try it!" But what they fail to realize is that it's what they're *not* eating that has the greatest impact.

A woman who eats fast food becomes a vegan. Of course she is going to feel better. A man goes from eating dairy and wheat at every meal to eating fruit. Of course he will feel better, too. They eliminated inflammatory foods. Their new diets aren't healing them; their vitality is coming forth after years of being tied up with inflammatory foods.

But should the vegan and the fruitarian continue on this dietary path long-term? Probably not. It was a positive experience, and they both learned something, but these ways of eating are not nutritionally sound over the long-term. And it's probably not just the diet that is healing them.

When people change their diet, they also usually

change other things in their lives. They might start sleeping more. Exercising more. Incorporating some stress reduction techniques into their world. But mark my words, these people are feeling better because of what they're not eating.

Eat the foods that Mother Nature provides, not man-made foods like cereal, soda, refined vegetable oils, high-fructose corn syrup, white flour, sugar, and processed cheese, just to name a few.

Yes, these man-made foods may taste good. Technology can sometimes fool your palate.

Yes, these man-made foods may also be convenient, but they come with a high cost. They fail to promote health and wellness, and they lower your vitality.

It's not about eating the right or wrong foods. It's about asking: how close to Nature am I?

Asking that single question moves us into the complexity of life and away from the good/bad and right/wrong way of thinking over and over and over again.

10. Do the best you can in the moment.

It is important to mention at this point that eating in peace is about choosing THE best food you can in that particular moment. At any given time, you have a spectrum of food choices. Somewhere between the ideal scenario, which is growing and hunting your own food, and the undesirable scenario of buying packaged, processed and man-made foods, is a non-obsessive, empowering way of eating.

Convenience foods will always be there. You have to make the choice.

Remember, this is about eating in peace, not eating in distress!

Your diet won't always be perfect. Eating in peace while traveling can be especially hard. One time at an airport, the best I could do was sliced turkey over a bed of lettuce. Definitely not the best meal I've ever had, but I avoided my food sensitivities and that made a difference in how I felt for the rest of my trip.

If you are traveling and all you can eat is food at an airport terminal or from a convenience store, use the spectrum of food choices to your advantage. Find the foods that come from nature. This might be a bag of nuts, jerky, or a piece of fruit. It may not always be ideal, but you can bless the food and move on with your day, knowing that you did the best you could.

You can plan ahead and pack your own snacks for your flight, of course, but sometimes life throws you a curve ball, and you need to be ready to surrender.

11. It's not what you do on Sunday that matters.

It's your habits that matter.

Eating in peace is an inspired lifestyle, of being present to your food and your body, and having fun along the way.

There is a time and place for everything.

On my last vacation on Maui, I ate something that I would never consume back home: Passion fruit sorbet.

Passion fruit is the taste of Aloha.

While it was gluten- and dairy-free, it did contain sugar—but only enough to bring out the incredible flavor. I loved every bite of it. I have no idea when and if I will ever have it again because my eating habits preclude eating sugar.

But on that day, I broke my habit. And it was wonderful. No regrets.

That is eating in peace.

There are sometimes in life, however, when I can't indulge. Sometimes straying from my diet plan won't work, and I will watch my family members eat the sorbet. The goal is always discernment. Asking the following question can bring clarity: how can I honor my highest good right here and right now?

That is eating in peace, too.

12. Where you spend money shows what you value.

Spend your money on real food. When you buy a soda, go to a fast-food restaurant, or buy a bag of candy or a bagel or a donut, you are communicating that something is ok when it isn't. What you decide to eat is bigger than you are.

As often as possible we need to choose foods based on their nutritional value, not their monetary cost.

It's not always easy. You might need to reallocate your

financial resources so you can afford good quality produce, meat, and fish. You might need to prioritize your
purchases. For example, if you eat eggs every morning,
seek out pastured eggs from the farmer's market. Identify
the things you eat most and make sure they are the best
quality possible.

If you examine your food budget and see that you are
spending a lot on wine, could you switch to less expensive ones or cut back on your consumption to free up some
funds for good food? Probably.

Eating in peace may require you to reallocate not only
your money, but your time and energy, too. A big part of
eating well is learning to cook. I don't want to be insensi-
tive to the demands of living in our modern world with
what I am about to say but the average person watches
television for 3 hours a day. Most meals take from 30 to
90 minutes to prepare. Come on! There are some very easy
recipes in the back of this book to help you in the kitchen.
Even if it's two or three meals a week, you can find some
time. You and your family are worth it.

When you spend money on good food and time preparing it for you and your family, you are in line with what
matters most—the sacred vessel of your body. Spirit wants
to express itself through you. Feed it well and it will serve
you well.

I have met numerous people who weren't willing to
change their ways for themselves, but when I ask about
their family, their spouse, and their children, they find the
motivation to do it for their loved ones.

The trick is to learn to love yourself as much as you love others.

13. Know thyself

Some people need to take baby steps; others need to have the rug pulled out from under them.

I for one think that moderation is for the birds. So many health professionals preach the 80/20 rule—do things "right" 80% of the time, and then you can play the other 20%. I urge you to be very careful with this rationalization. Yes, moderation can work for many, many people, and if it does, consider yourself blessed. But for many others, moderation can be the beginning of the end. Tell an alcoholic to drink in moderation. It doesn't work. As I said earlier, sometimes an extreme situation deserves an extreme intervention.

Many 12-step programs preach ODAT —one day at a time. In other words, don't trouble yourself about the long term. Focus only on today. Tomorrow, you'll worry about tomorrow. It's a strategy that keeps people from getting overwhelmed by the magnitude of their goal, and encourages them to celebrate and draw strength from each small victory.

When teaching people to eat in peace, I encourage them to live OMAT—one meal at a time.

Set yourself up for success and be practical with your efforts to change. This guideline comes from one of my favorite nutrition and herbal teachers, Paul Bergner.

First, add foods.

Second, replace foods.

Third, remove foods.

Here is a concrete example of adding food. A few years ago, a client gave me her diet diary. Her primary beverages were tea and diet soda. Instead of replacing or removing these, I said, "I want you to drink half your body weight in water." When she agreed to that, her increased water intake pushed out the other beverages.

Then, there is replacement. Sometimes I recommend that someone stop drinking diet sodas and start drinking coffee again. Once again, diet sodas are a man-made metabolic disaster. Not only do they contain synthetic caffeine removed from what nature intended, but artificial sweeteners, which are also toxic.

Removing foods can often be the last option and the most difficult for people to follow. In the case of chronic inflammatory disease, this is where addressing food sensitivities comes in. Let's take out the inflammatory foods, like wheat, dairy, corn, and soy, and see how your experience of life and your body shift.

Eating one meal at a time, and adding, replacing, and removing foods, are viable strategies for making effective, long-term dietary changes.

All who wander are not lost.

Congratulations!

You've made it this far, and now have a framework for

what and how to eat. If you wander off the Eat in Peace path, it is ok. Do not throw in the towel. Just decide to return to these principles at your very next meal.

As I write this, we are at the beginning of a new year. This time can be a powerful motivator to make fresh resolutions about changing our lives, and our diets in particular. I sometimes get torn between the hype of New Year's and the realization that it's just another day. I used to make really BIG promises to myself at New Year's, thinking something magical was in store and I would somehow become a new person. Not so much! My practice now as the new year approaches is not one of resolutions but of reflection, asking what the past year of my life taught me, and what I want to create from that.

During this time of year, I see people get caught up in unproductive conversations about their health and fitness goals. It's time to get that gym membership (that you're not going to use)! Or it's time to do that cleanse! The reality is that while the new year can offer motivation to change, we must realize that it's our choices in each moment that define us. It's always back to the basics, like what you are going to choose for breakfast this morning. Don't make promises you can't keep. Don't think, "I'm going to start eating well on Monday" (that was my old favorite). The only sane thing to do is live for right now—make the best decision you can at this moment to bring forth your vitality. So yes, let's use the energy of the new year as a time for reflection. That's what the winter is for: a quiet time to think. But don't forget that every moment is a new beginning.

Do not confuse simple with easy. This is a practice. Eating in peace requires dedication, planning, and vigilance, but the rewards are astounding, and the benefits spread into all areas of your life.

What you feed your mind is just as important as what you feed your body.

Your eyes are like the mouth of your nervous system. Your eyes ingest the world around you and then, your nervous system has to digest whatever you take in. Therefore, what you read and what you watch create you as much as what you eat.

I grew up watching soap operas and horror movies, which taught me that people are manipulative and that life is scary. These days, aside from selected movies and shows on Netflix, we don't watch television in our house, and we don't use screens as a babysitter for our son. Now scary and violent movies make me nauseous, and I see that as a sign of good health. In our modern world, too many people watch stories as opposed to living them. Get out there and create your own.

And then, of course, there is what your skin eats.

In an ideal world, I wouldn't put anything on my skin that I wouldn't eat, because here's the deal: what you put on your skin is directly absorbed into your bloodstream. This is important to understand because when something goes through your digestive tract, the liver starts its detoxification process BEFORE it goes into the bloodstream. So that means when you slather creams onto your skin, put on make-up, and use toxic hair-care products, you dramatically increase your toxic burden.

Besides, healthy skin is an inside job. You don't glow from the outside; you glow from the inside.

The same thing goes for cleaning supplies, and don't even get me started on antibacterial soaps and hand sanitizers.

Your body is eating and digesting everything in your environment. Be mindful.

No one left behind

I cannot think of a single illness that could not be eased by eating in peace. If a child or family member wants to heal through food, do not ostracize them from your dining-room table or make fun of them. Being sick is hard enough. Rally around them and change with them. EVERYONE is better off eating the whole foods that Mother Nature intended. It is the epitome of preventative medicine and a powerful intervention for chronic disease patterns. Illness is one of the most transformative experiences available to us. A sick family member is a platform for changing your life; that way, everyone wins.

Also, maintain your integrity. Beware of dietary fads. Study the new fad and see if it makes good sense. When something new comes along, wait five years and see if it stands the test of time.

You can also hold up the fad to the light of Mother Nature. Does it make good sense in terms of what we know about how our ancestors lived?

The intelligence of the entire universe is within you.

Your body does not care what you look like. Whether you have acne or a chronic rash, whether you hate your hair or your shape or your face, your body is smarter than you will ever be. Trust that it is right for you, as uncomfortable or unattractive as that may be at times. Face the fact that you only have two options here: hate and disrespect, or love and respect. Choose the latter. Love will move you towards healing. Start loving yourself wherever and however you can and that love will grow.

Food has a lot to do with our vitality. It is not everything, but it is a BIG part of the picture. When vitality declines, this is often labeled as a disease. Outside the roughly 2% of the population with congenital conditions, disease is preventable and largely caused by lifestyle choices. Consider that disease is dis-ease.

There is only adaptation.

There is nothing to fix.

There is nothing wrong.

The only question to ask is: what has my body been adapting to?

I thought I had asthma for 30 years. I now know I never had asthma. The current medical model failed me.

I had difficulty breathing because I had a dairy sensitivity that was only discovered when I removed that food group from my diet. That food is not a part of my life anymore. It never will be, and I am more than ok with that because I breathe easy. Life without dairy is good.

In a flash, I was able to let go of my painful past. All those years of carrying around my inhaler, which I called my Puffer. All those years of feeling defective because I couldn't breathe without medicine. There was nothing EVER wrong with me! NOTHING! My body was just adapting to what I was eating and how I was living.

Isn't that liberating?

But the flip side of being liberated is responsibility. You are responsible for caring for your body. You are responsible for what you put in your mouth. So stop making excuses and figure out what you need to do to be the most vital version of yourself.

The only thing you ever need to ask yourself before eating a food is: does this food exist in nature? Is it real food? Once you determine the answer, then your body will decide if that food is good for you or not. All you have to do is pay attention.

You are looking for foods that make your body sing. It is hard to find words for this. It is a feeling. A sensing. A knowing without knowing.

If the answer is yes, this food serves me, inquire deeper.

If the answer is no, this food does not serve me, inquire deeper.

Maybe a theme will emerge that can teach you something about your body.

I decreased saturated fats in my life for years, thinking that they were bad for me. Now I thrive on fatty foods and protein. My carbohydrate metabolism is beyond repair after years of eating sugar, and I just don't feel good after eating carbohydrate-rich foods. This may or may not be true for you, but you are sure to find out as you start to listen to your body.

This isn't about whether you like or dislike a food, but rather, does this food bring forth my vitality? If so, why? If not, why not? Why does this food impede my vitality?

Give that little voice within you the time and space it needs to speak. And then, that voice will speak to you about other areas of life. It might sound something like this: "Hey, now that I am eating the real foods that Nature provides and I am feeling alive, how come I'm not happier? Oh, it's because this person over here is sucking my life force away. Time to let that person go." Trust me, another person will find you, one who adds to your life rather than drains it.

I used to have a number of toxic friendships with people who made fun of me for my food issues and put me down as a hypochondriac. Not any more. If someone does not make me feel more alive and safe in this world, then I spend as little time as possible with them.

So it goes with places, jobs, decisions, and so on. When you embrace intuitive eating, you invite intuitive living.

Eating whole foods places you in the universal matrix of life, where you will find vitality.

If you crave structure, please read Your Eat-in-Peace Plate, where you will find a list of foods to emphasize.

CHAPTER 3

DRINK IN PEACE

*"The cure for anything is salt water:
sweat, tears, and the sea."*

—ISAK DINESEN

We all breathe, pee, sweat, and poop.

These are the detoxification pathways: our lungs, our urinary tract, our sweat glands and our digestive tract. What unites them?

Water.

In order to keep these detoxification pathways moving, they must be wet.

How much water should you consume? Drink when you're thirsty (and eat when you're hungry). Your body talks to you all the time. Listen to it. Unfortunately, many people suffer from chronic dehydration and mistake thirst for hunger. Drinking half your body weight in ounces is a general rule of thumb to understand what hydration feels like.

Lots of people ask me about what kind of water filter to buy. To be honest, I don't know. There are so many options it makes me dizzy, and some are super expensive. My family uses a Berkey water filter, and we love it. We buy as little bottled water as possible because the plastic compounds mimic hormones and wreak havoc with your health and the health of the entire planet (the earth can't digest plastic). What I can say for sure is drink water. Drink it in all forms. Green tea is fantastic. Herbal teas are great. Kombuchas and kefirs are good for most people.

If your thirst is persistent despite drinking adequate water, consider adding a half-teaspoon of good quality salt, with a twist of lime or lemon, to a 16-oz glass of water morning and night. I like to rotate Celtic, Redmond Real Salt, and pink salt from Premier Research Labs, as each one has a different mineral profile. This is actually a good self-care practice for anyone, particularly if you are following a low-carbohydrate diet or are physically active. Salt is not a condiment; it is a necessary nutrient. If you have demonized salt, then I highly recommend reading *The Salt Fix* by James DiNicolantonio.

Next step: eliminate ice. Room temperature to warm water is more effective than ice-cold water for reasons we'll explore in the next chapter. Of course you should enjoy a nice cold beverage every now and then, but I wouldn't recommend that you make it a regular affair. You want to stoke your digestive fire, not put it out with ice.

Also, please eat your calories, don't drink them. Most bottled teas, sodas, and beverages are loaded with sweeteners and add nothing to your health in return.

Remember, you want to stay as close to nature as possible. Nature doesn't juice. The fiber present in fruits and vegetables is your friend. When you press it out, all you're left with is the resulting sugar. That said, juice can be a lovely, cooling beverage in the heat of the summer. Just be sure to add back a little fiber, along with a teaspoon or two of high-quality oil, like olive or flax, to help with the absorption of fat-soluble nutrients. Or as I learned from Amanda Love's Nourishing Cleanse program, you can juice your vegetables and then use a blender to add in an avocado. Any of these additions will increase the complexity of the juice.

One more tip: chew your smoothies. Chewing turns on your digestive function. So put some ground flax seeds on top or add some chopped nuts or berries, and chow down.

No conversation about water and hydration would be complete without discussing America's two favorite beverages: coffee and alcohol.

"Coffee keeps you awake until it's acceptable to drink wine." —A billboard

I'd spent the past few years defending coffee, until I stopped drinking it and realized how it was affecting my body.

Let me back up and say that my relationship to stimulants started when I was just a baby. If you can recall from my story, I ate a lot of sugar. Sugar is a stimulant. Then I started using my Albuterol inhaler regularly, which is another stimulant. As I started competing in triathlons, I turned to Red Bulls and caffeinated energy goo packs. Then, I started to understand health and filled my days up with three to four cups of green tea. When I became a parent, however, I realized tea wasn't going to cut it and I started drinking coffee. I started drinking it just once or twice per day when I needed to improve my mental or physical performance, but soon enough, that was every day.

I share this because I want you to see that the use of drugs in our food supply escalates. Over 40 years of life, I needed more and more caffeine to get my hit, until finally I started to get heart palpitations. I noticed that I was more intense than usual, on the verge of just being angry and irritable all the time. I had intense moments of existential angst and felt like I was going to simply implode.

I put two and two together and thought, "Is all this from coffee?" That deep voice inside me said, "Yep." So I started to reduce my coffee intake by a half cup each week. In three weeks, I was caffeine free. What did I notice?

My sleep greatly improved. It was easier to fall asleep and my sleep was deeper. I woke up feeling more alert.

A sense of calm replaced my feelings of impending doom.

My energy was more stable and came from a deeper place.

Carbohydrate cravings decreased dramatically.

I was a more patient mother and a happier partner.

I felt more flow and freedom, like my well-being wasn't dependent on a beverage.

My menstrual cycle was smooth as silk. No sugar cravings. No mood swings. No discomforts.

I was able to prioritize my tasks more effectively and efficiently. Coffee had made me feel like everything was so important!

I didn't need so many relaxing, nervine herbs (more on that later). I was literally using herbal medicine throughout the day to address coffee-induced anxiety.

And this is the most important realization of all: I observed that I never needed more energy; I needed more awareness.

As long as I was masking my fatigue with caffeinated beverages, I wasn't aware of what I needed in any given moment. Now, sometimes in the afternoon, I feel a wave a fatigue come over me and it feels healthy! I do what I can in the moment to slow down, or even lie down, and I find myself much more refreshed for the rest of the day.

Also, your life force wants to flow, unimpeded, through your body. I'm just not sure that coffee facilitates this free movement of energy. For me, it created tension in my muscles, which I often describe as that "shoulders are up to my ears" phenomenon. I am clearly better without it.

I mean, who needs more stress?

And it wasn't just about my physical body, it was also about my emotional experience. If coffee makes me angry and intense, then how do I know how I really feel about something? I don't!

It took me 41 years to get here, to arrive at a place where I wanted to feel my body on its own, where I could trust myself in a whole new way, without stimulants.

So let's talk about how caffeine works.

Notice I did not say, let's talk about how coffee works. Many health professionals talk about coffee and caffeine as if they are the same thing. They are not.

Caffeine works by blocking adenosine receptors in the brain. Adenosine signals fatigue. You feel tired. You consume caffeine and then you don't feel tired anymore.

You will hear nutritionists say that caffeine will ruin your adrenal glands. That's an oversimplification. Caffeine is an enabler. By taking the brakes off of fatigue, there is a potential to over-exert yourself, but if you are well rested, drink caffeine in moderation, and don't push yourself, then, well, you can drink your coffee in peace.

If you want to learn more about this subject, read Murray Carpenter's book *Caffeinated*.

I wouldn't touch synthetic caffeine with a ten-foot pole. It is completely against what Mother Nature ever intended for our bodies.

The caffeine added to drinks and foods is not a plant extract. It is made in a laboratory. It is a synthetic powder made in China and is used in sodas and other processed crap. It lacks the integrity of what nature intended for our bodies. Numerous deaths have been reported from energy drinks containing synthetic caffeine[3]; no one dies of coffee consumption. Experts speculate that there may be protective compounds in coffee, or that when caffeine is consumed in its natural form, your body tells you, "You've had enough." This may show up as stomach upset or you may simply start to feel weird.

So is coffee inherently bad?

Hell no.

Coffee is a powerful herbal medicine. Anything that is powerful has a tendency to polarize people, including health professionals. This is why some claim that coffee is a miracle cure for all that ails us, and other health professionals demonize it. Our minds want to make coffee right or wrong, but life doesn't work like that. Context is everything.

Here are a few examples of how coffee is beneficial.

For people who live in areas where a convenience store is the only grocery store, a cup of coffee may be the most antioxidants their body sees all day long. Coffee's rich, dark color indicates that it is full of protective compounds.

Coffee is also high in chlorogenic acid, which plays a positive role in blood sugar regulation. It actually helps insulin work more effectively on a cellular level. So for someone with insulin resistance or Type II diabetes, coffee could be a very appropriate beverage.

Coffee may also be appropriate for vasodilatory headaches. These are headaches where often the head feels hot. The person may look flushed. It may hurt to bend down, and there is a natural inclination to want to put something cold on the head. Caffeine constricts blood vessels and may help bring the body back into balance.

Along the same lines, coffee is powerful medicine for people who may be overly affected by low-pressure weather systems, when the air is heavy and damp. A person might also feel heavy and damp and sluggish, and for lack of a better word, depressed, with low energy. Coffee can restore balance, bring a sense of lightness back into the body, and facilitate joy.

I have also worked with a handful of clients who stopped drinking coffee and started drinking diet sodas because they thought the latter was healthier. By now, you know the truth! I immediately recommend returning to coffee. Diet sodas have no place in our food supply.

So how can you best enjoy your cup of coffee? Here are some guidelines.

- Buy organic and fair trade whenever possible. These are both better for the environment and for your body.

- Find a local roaster and grind your own beans. This ensures good quality and taste. The minute coffee (or any spice or herb) is ground it begins to lose is volatile components, which often contain medicine.

- DO NOT EVER use imitation cream, low-fat dairy, or any other toxic sludge in your coffee. Coffee, like all plants, is sacred. Please don't disrespect it with weird, man-made additives.
- Learn to like black coffee, because when you travel sometimes you just can't find the good cream.
- Consider making butter coffee, which includes one tablespoon of butter from pastured cows, one table-spoon of unrefined coconut oil, and an optional scoop of collagen protein, with a dash of vanilla. Blend until smooth in a high-speed blender and you have an amazing latte!
- While I encourage you to avoid sweeteners in your coffee, if you must, use small amounts of natural sweet-eners like stevia, maple syrup, honey, coconut sugar, or xylitol, and forgo artificial sweeteners and sugar.

Please remember that, as with all things, some people do well on coffee and others don't. You have to figure out which you are.

If it makes you feel good and your sleep is sufficient, enjoy.

If it makes you jittery or upsets your stomach, avoid it.

Alcohol is just like coffee.

Again: some people do well on it, others not so much.

I am biased when it comes to alcohol. I come from

a family of alcoholics. I have witnessed the full spectrum, from highly functional alcoholics to those who have lost everything and live on the street. Three years into my healing journey, I realized that alcohol was no longer serving my highest good. Its effects were unpredictable on my emotional body, and it elicited an inflammatory cascade on my physical body that was difficult to recover from. I was using it to calm my nerves at the end of the day, but it wasn't helping my vitality anymore. So I made a decision not to drink alcohol, and I feel much better for it.

You may be different. I think a glass of wine or beer, or a cocktail, can be medicinal for many people. Alcohol is a blood mover, which is why the herbal medicines I love are water and alcohol extracts. You know those rosy cheeks you get with a good drink? That feeling of warmth from a hot toddy? Yep, that's your blood moving. Stagnant blood is no good. All of life wants to move.

Alcohol is also a social beverage and makes many people feel relaxed and happy. Nothing wrong with that, in moderation, either.

As far as what types of alcohol are best, it's going to depend. I am partial to wine or beer. Just listen to your body. There is no need to make this complicated. Drink what makes you feel good, and don't drink so much you feel lousy the next day.

Do be aware, however, of sugar and carbohydrates. Alcohol contains sugar and can negatively impact your blood sugar and liver function. If you are working on decreasing refined carbohydrates in your diet, then there's not much place for alcohol.

I have met far too many recovered alcoholics who morph into sugar and carbohydrate addicts. They stopped drinking their sugar, so now they eat it. The sad thing is that this prevents them from feeling free from the alcohol. Their bodies have learned to associate the sugar rush with alcohol, so they continue to want it. They are hindering their recovery.

Also, alcohol affects your judgment. You may decide to stay up late or eat an inflammatory food, neither of which is in your best interest during your healing process.

A word to the wise

For many people, coffee and alcohol are daily rituals that mark important transition points during the day. We use caffeine to wake up in the morning; we use alcohol to relax in the evening.

Caffeine is a stimulant.

Alcohol is a depressant.

Both are drugs that can exert both positive and negative influences on the body. Which drugs you tend toward tells an entire story about who you are and where you might need more support. It is not by accident that we drink caffeine to start our days and alcohol to end them. As you get healthy and learn to facilitate your vitality, these beverages are less likely to be a form of self-medication. You might begin to enjoy them for the brief shift in consciousness that they provide.

Or you may find that you really don't need them at all because you feel fully alive on your own.

You see, drugs are everywhere in our modern world: prescription drugs, recreational drugs, sugar, caffeine, and alcohol.

One of the questions I ask my clients is about their recreational drug use. Sometimes people will reveal a strong preference for depressants, such as alcohol and marijuana. Some people say, "Oh yeah, I used to be hooked on amphetamines," or "Back in the day, cocaine was my drug of choice." This information can be very helpful in terms of knowing yourself and being healthy.

Coffee shops, liquor stores, and bars are around every corner and are often very busy establishments, right? We use these substances to help us move through our days. We use them to shift the state of our nervous systems, to either heighten our arousal or dampen it. Coffee and alcohol become coping strategies.

"Save me from myself!" we scream. "Where is my cup of coffee? Where is my glass of wine?"

I am here to tell you that you have healthier alternatives.

In the words of Rudolf Steiner, "For every human illness, somewhere in the world exists a plant which is the cure."

Herbs and vitality

I want to be very clear that the herbs I'm about to discuss are not drugs.

In his book *The Consultation in Phytotherapy: The Herbal Practitioner's Approach to the Patient*, Peter Conway put together a chart explaining the difference between herbs and drugs.

Herbal Medicine	Pharmaceutical Drug
Slow	Rapid
Subtle	Crude
Gentle	Aggressive
Familiar	Alien
Complex	Simple
Food-like	"Un-like"
General	Precise
Total	Partial
Diffuse	Targeted
Natural	Synthetic
Messy	Tidy
Chaotic	Ordered
Attractive	Repulsive
From-life	Non-life
Feminine	Masculine[4]

When an herb interacts with our physiology, it nudges hundreds of pathways, activating some and de-activating others. It is dancing with you! With pharmaceutical drugs, there is no dance; there is only suppression of these pathways.

The appropriate use of drugs may *save* your life, but they do not *create* life. Herbs, however, can decrease our dependency on sugar, alcohol, and caffeine. If we incorporated more herbs into our diets, our bodies would be more vital and we would feel less stressed.

I have clients who are hesitant or completely resistant to the use of herbal medicine. I also have the pleasure of teaching holistic health professionals who are scared of herbal medicine. They actually say, "Herbs are like drugs. You gotta be careful."

REALLY?!

Drugs are a modern invention; plants have been here since the beginning of time. Have you heard the biblical story of the Three Wise Men, bringing gifts of gold, frankincense, and myrrh to the birth of Jesus? The latter two are herbs.

How did we become so casual about the use of prescription and over-the-counter drugs, and so scared of the plant medicines that our bodies evolved on?

Actually, I can answer that question.

First, Big Pharma has spent a lot of money brainwashing people to believe that humans can make medicines better than Mother Nature.

Second, our fears of nature run deep, and rightly so. Yes,

there are poisonous plants out there, and natural catastrophes happen, but we can't continue to protect ourselves at the expense of cutting ourselves off from the healing tools only found in the wild. We should respect the tool, not fear it. Nature isn't out to get us; it is out to heal us. Life is on our side! We need to work with it, not fight it.

What we have come to accept as normal is a unique form of insanity.

I wouldn't be here today without inhalers, steroids, and antibiotics. I spent twenty-plus years of my life ingesting artificial foods and combating the terrible symptoms that they created with artificial drugs.

Am I grateful that Western medicine kept me alive? Yes, but my inhalers didn't get me WELL! If I had identified my food sensitivities, learned how to eat real food, and incorporated herbs into my diet early on, I wouldn't have suffered, and I wouldn't have needed drugs.

Drugs aren't normal. Drugs aren't healing. They should be a last resort, not a first line of defense. While they kept my physical body alive, they did nothing for my spirit, other than take me down a deep dark hole that I had to climb out of to create the person that I am today.

Following a class I taught about blending liquid herbs I received a message from one of the attendees, who said that "studying herbal nutrition had never been so fun."

Herbal nutrition. I had never heard that phrase before, but damn, it's a good one! One of the reasons so many Americans suffer from chronic inflammatory diseases is that our bodies are starving for herbal plant material as much as—if not more than—they are for real food, along with clean water and air.

You may be alive without the use of herbal nutrition, but you won't be FULLY alive! And I am interested in teaching people to be fully alive.

"But herbs taste yucky!"

That's not their fault. See, plants can't move. They have to adapt to their environment or die. For instance, when cows graze alfalfa, the alfalfa makes more tannins, which don't taste all that great, so the cow starts to move along to graze somewhere else. Herbs adapt by making phytochemicals called secondary metabolites. These compounds may be bitter or astringent and may push away predators.

Mother Nature is brilliant! We benefit greatly from these secondary metabolites, but because they don't taste so great, we deprive our bodies of their benefits.

You won't find these secondary metabolites listed on a nutritional label, but it doesn't mean that you don't need them!

Your nervous system and herbs

Western herbalists like myself define herbs by their actions—in other words, their effects on your body that weren't there before.

A useful way to think about this is that nutrition relates to structure in the body, and herbs relate to function. In other words, food determines what your body is made out of and herbs ask your body to do something. They work best together!

The classification of herbs I want to discuss here is nervine tonics, which are defined as substances that improve the tone, vigor, and function of the nervous system. Nervine tonics both relax and energize the nervous system.

That last statement is essential to understanding the power of herbal medicine. Hopefully, you can recall a time when you felt simultaneously both relaxed and energized? Maybe you were camping, or at the movies with friends, or sitting around a table talking at a dinner party. To me, this feeling of being both calm and alert is the ultimate state of vitality and aliveness. I am going to share three of my favorite nervines with you that may help elicit this feeling. Start ingesting these, and you might find that, while you still enjoy caffeine and alcohol, you will be less likely to use them on a daily basis to self-medicate.

1. Schisandra chinensis berry

I love this herb so much that I used to joke about naming my child Schisandra if I had a girl, but I had to come up with another idea when I gave birth to a boy!

Schisandra is the herb of five tastes. It is bitter, sweet, salty, pungent, and sour. The more complex the taste, the more complex the medicine.

Schisandra is a prime example of an herb that offers a polypharmacy where your body gets to choose its medicine. Not only does it relax the nervous system and energize the endocrine system, it is very supportive of liver detoxification.

It is fantastic for people who work with a lot of chemicals, like hairdressers, manicurists, painters, factory workers, and auto mechanics.

I also consider it an herb for containment. It is for people who may cry too much, sweat too much, or are overly expressive. Overall, the schisandra person is leaky and just doesn't hold on to his/her fluids very well.

If you are really tuned into the conversation here, you may be wondering: how can an herb detoxify, which essentially means letting things go, AND contain, which means holding things in? The majority of herbs are amphoteric or biphasic, meaning that they can work in both directions, and your body decides what it needs. The plant has the ability to normalize functions.

On that note, it is important to remember that anxiety and depression are different sides of the same coin, which is a dysregulated nervous system that can't respond to life in a healthy way, alternating between being overly excited and insufficiently stimulated. Schisandra is a wonderful ally for smoothing out those rough waters. It introduces stability into the body without making you feel sedated or overly stimulated, and addresses the chronic inflammation that is the underlying cause of anxiety and depression.

Through its positive effects on the stress response and inflammation, it also promotes mental clarity and regulates appetite, particularly for people who may be overeating.

I remember when I first started making Liver Love,

which is a schisandra and honey concoction, one of my clients called me and said, "Oh my God. I'm not overeating anymore! I make my dinner plate, like I always do, but I stop eating half way." I must admit that during the conversation I smiled and nodded, and was sort of dismissive, like, ok, that's nice. But then two other clients called and told me the same thing. All three women were perimenopausal and struggling to make that hormonal transition. Schisandra helped.

Then there are those who get stressed and don't eat. It helps those people, too. How? The same way it can calm an over-reactive nervous system and excite a different one. The same way that it both detoxifies and contains resources. It normalizes functions, including appetite.

There are a few ways to enjoy schisandra.

You can find a video on how to make Liver Love, my schisandra and honey combination, on my website. The moistening quality of honey offsets the astringent/drying properties of schisandra, so this is a good way to take schisandra long-term.

Some people keep a small bowl of the dried berries on their desk to nibble on throughout the day.

Roughly 20 berries equal a gram.

About 2–4 grams per day is the dose.

You can purchase organic berries through bulk herb vendors like Pacific Botanicals and Mountain Rose Herbs.

I also like the liquid extract from MediHerb, Schisandra 1:2. It combines nicely with herbs like astragalus, eleuthero, and licorice for people who need endocrine, nervous, and immune system support.

2. Passiflora incarnata aerial parts

Passion flower is one of the most beautiful flowers you will ever find. It is nothing short of spectacular. No matter how many times I see it, it always mesmerizes me, and reminds me that we are not alone, or even in charge. This flower is an expression of the Divine.

It is important to pay attention to how plants grow, because sometimes the plant's way of being in the world communicates something about its use. Passion flower is a vine. It moves slowly, with strength. It flows. Passion flower's primary use is as a mild sedative. It calms the nervous system and the mind. In fact, passion flower is particularly beneficial to people who suffer from circular, obsessive thinking patterns and are overall tense in their musculature.

I remember the first time I experienced the effects of passion flower. I often clenched my fist under the dinner table. As I ate with my right hand, my left hand would make a fist under the table, ready to fight! But after a dose of passion flower, all of a sudden I noticed my left hand just resting in my lap. My fist was gone.

Passion flower is a very gentle remedy that can be used all day to support a tired, easily triggered nervous system. Many people looking for sleep remedies don't realize that what you do (or don't do) in the morning affects how you sleep. For the most part, if you want better sleep at night, you need to relax during the day. Relaxing herbs like passion flower can help.

I like the passion flower from Galen's Way. Take 2 ml, three to four times a day, diluted in water.

3. Piper mythisticum root

Piper mythisticum is called kava kava, which means "talk talk." This plant comes to us from the Pacific Islands.

Not all kava is created equal. I have tried a lot of it over the years, and I did not think it was the herb for me. It gave me frontal headaches, and made me feel dull overall, sometimes relaxing my body, yet stimulating my mind. It was an uncomfortable experience. Then, a few years ago, a company from Australia called MediHerb came out with a product called Kava Forte. I reluctantly tried it one day when I was feeling particularly anxious, and what happened surprised me.

A sense of peace washed over me. I felt physically relaxed and present. I felt happy. It was wonderful.

Once again, quality is everything when it comes to herbal medicine. You have to have superior plant material and then process it in a way that brings out the best of that particular herb. MediHerb nailed it.

I remember when my mom first tried it. She had come to visit us when our son Drake was a baby. She was 72 at the time and lived 45 miles away. Her sister had just died and she was distraught, anxious, and grieving. As she was leaving she started crying, so I told her to come back in and sit down at the table. I gave her a Kava Forte tablet to chew. It numbed her tongue, which is what good-quality kava does, and I watched her relax. She started breathing deeply, and felt ready to make her drive home.

I told her to call me when she got home. When she did, she said, "What is that stuff you gave me, Charlotte? I mean, really, that is good shit. It was like having a scotch on the rocks with lunch with none of the fatigue or sluggishness. Cars were driving by so fast, and it didn't bother me. I feel so calm, like, everything is going to be ok."

Clearly my mom made a connection on her own about kava and alcohol. I mentioned earlier that I stopped drinking alcohol years ago when I realized that it triggered an inflammatory state in my body. I have been much better off without it. There are many clinicians who recommend kava for people who may be drinking too much alcohol. Once again, if the body can find balance with an herbal ally, then the need to self-medicate with drugs declines. The wonderful thing about kava is that an appropriate dose does not diminish reflexes or mental clarity the way that alcohol and marijuana can.

I know many parents who chew a kava on their way home from work so that they don't walk into their homes stressed out from their day. Then, they can greet their children and spouse with love and more patience. Coming home from work to your family is not an easy transition for the nervous system to make!

I haven't seen alcohol help. Alcohol contributes to emotional volatility and anger, while kava makes you a better version of yourself.

I once attended a big meeting where I felt a bit nervous and out of my comfort zone, which caused me to be withdrawn. On the last day, I was really challenged by a presentation, and I felt that invisible punch to my stomach. I was slightly nauseous, with butterflies floating in my belly, so I chewed a kava tablet and felt myself come back into my body. That was the expected result, but here was the surprise. At lunch that day, I was talkative. I wanted to connect with other people! I felt like me! Kava brought me back to myself.

I never thought of myself as having social anxiety, but kava has taught me that I do carry more stress than I thought when I'm around people I don't know, and it helps me move through that. Herbs can teach us things about ourselves that we didn't know!

Another time, when Drake was a baby, we both had the flu. There is only one thing more miserable than being sick, and that's being sick while caring for a sick infant. It is just awful. After a few days, I stopped sleeping because I just hurt all over. I was so tense. One night after putting Drake to sleep, I stood in the kitchen with my head in my hands, not knowing what to do next. Then, I looked up and saw a bottle of Kava Forte. I thought, "I've got nothing to lose here." I took a tablet, chewed it, and started breathing calmly again. It was extraordinary. I got into bed and slept all night long, and my fever broke. I do not think of kava for immune support, but it profoundly shifted my nervous system from a tense state to a relaxed one, so that my immune system could do its job.

There are so many stories I could tell. I use kava all the time now. It is a very spiritual plant for me, and helps to bring me into the present moment.

Never underestimate the power of an herb. They are underutilized tools for better living. In the recipe section in the back of this book, you will find a recipe for kava coladas. It is an amazing beverage for your self-care and natural medicine cabinet.

Always remember, quality is key. Kava Forte from Medi-Herb is a water extraction, the way our ancestors prepared it. This is distinct from many of the water and alcohol extracts on the market. It is also sourced from what is called a noble cultivar. This refers to how our ancestors selected plant material. The medicine man would go out into the field and taste the herb, looking for a specific effect. Over time, that kava with an identifiable phytochemical profile became the prized plant material, the one you could count on.

Kava is a well-studied herb. There is a lot of science to back up how it affects brain chemistry and eases pain, along with relaxing the nervous system and skeletal muscle. (If you are a health professional interested in the more technical aspects of this plant, please read the chapter on kava in the 2nd edition of *Principles & Practices of Phytotherapy,* by Kerry Bone and Simon Mills.)

Now that we've discussed food and beverages, the next logical topic is digestion, the home of your second brain.

CHAPTER 4

POOP IN PEACE

"Never trust a skinny cook
or anyone who says they don't fart."

—ME

Picture this: I follow my three-and-a-half year old son into the bathroom the other day. He walks through the door, grabs the handle, turns around and says, "I am going to close this door, Mommy, ok? I want to poop in peace. Bye-bye!"

Where did he learn *that*?

Potty humor aside, there is no way that I could write about vitality without dedicating a chapter to digestion. You can't have one without the other. That is a recurring theme throughout this book: nothing exists in isolation. So if you have a digestive disturbance, like heartburn, gas, constipation, or diarrhea, I have already discussed four key areas that will help you get to the core of your digestive distress: address what you eat *and* how you eat it, stay hydrated, and tend to your nervous system.

When I first started my clinical training as an herbalist, a woman at one of my talks told me her husband *had* to come see me. Usually that is a recipe for disaster, because the spouse couldn't care less and comes under duress. But this situation was different. This guy, whom we'll call Jed, was having a tough time. He was 27 years old and described his bowel movements as icebergs coming out of his butt. EEK! Here is his story in his own words:

> When I first started working with Charlotte I had terrible abdominal pain. Nearly every one of my joints ached (from neck, back, and ankles, and everywhere in between); my skin was flaky; and I often had varying bouts of constipation

and diarrhea. My asthma had gotten so bad that I remember standing in the rain in a parking lot while waiting for a table at a restaurant, and I was coughing violently from cigarette smoke from someone I could not even see. Over the past 5 years I had seen many physicians, including but not limited to family and internal medicine, dermatologists (who found four different rashes of unknown origin on my body), gastroenterologists, a neurologist, and had made multiple visits to the ER for pain and or bleeding from the bowels. I had multiple CT scans, ultrasounds, X-rays, an MRI, 2 endoscopies, and a colonoscopy. Over the past three or four years I had become accustomed to taking a Claritin every day (March through at least October), and several different pain medicines (Aleve, Advil, Tylenol, even Lortab occasionally). I also had a daily routine of caking on at least one or two lotions to stop the flaking and itching. The pain in my joints was by far the most unbearable, and this past winter brought pain that I cannot even describe. I thought I was going to die. I had given up exercise completely, including biking, which even last summer I was able to perform regularly. In addition to all of the other ailments, I had actually given myself an ulcer by taking too much pain medicine. Of all my doctors' exams and tests, this was the only solid diagnosis I was ever given. All of this trouble had occurred before my 28th birthday.

During our first consultation, I asked Jed and his wife if anyone had discussed his diet with him, and as I suspected, no one had. After looking at his diet diary, I suggested an elimination diet. An elimination diet is the gold standard for uncovering food sensitivities. Over six weeks, you remove the most common food allergens, like wheat, dairy, corn, and soy, from your diet.

So how did we figure out that gluten was the culprit? All Jed had to do was observe his body. After a few week of being gluten-free, I asked him to tell me how he felt:

> I have now been gluten-free since June and what a difference that has made! My stomach no longer hurts, and I have regular bowel movements. My skin has cleared up completely. A couple of weeks ago, I waited for a bus in one of those enclosed bus stop shelters while someone (sitting right beside me) smoked. I felt great and didn't cough once—my lungs didn't burn at all. I no longer have any need to take Claritin, as my allergies have all but gone away. I no longer wake up with pain in my joints; in fact, I have actually been going back to the gym and was able to get there six days last week without pain or the need of an inhaler. I feel normal. I can't remember ever feeling as good as I feel right now. I was

diagnosed with asthma at age 13 and have had rashes and allergies as long as I can remember. I can't thank Charlotte enough for just taking the time to listen and for actually looking at the whole picture. Conventional medicine is so compartmentalized that physicians, whether out of fear or lack of training, only look at one piece and expect to solve the puzzle.

This man had spent over $10,000 in the medical system.

You know how much he paid me in student clinic? Fifty bucks.

I can't decide if this difference in cost excites me or makes me want to vomit in disgust. Probably a little bit of both.

Start with the obvious

Now we go full circle. If you are not pooping in peace and suffer from digestive disturbances, your first point of inquiry should be the food you are eating. That power is in your hands. Sure, speak to a holistic health professional and get some support. But don't hand over your power to a medical doctor who is untrained in nutrition, where you will potentially waste thousands of dollars and be no better off than you were before you started.

The first thing to ask is, am I eating real food?

Remember, real food is defined as whole foods from nature that most closely resemble what our ancestors ate.

If you can say yes, then you know your discomfort isn't a reaction to artificial dyes, preservatives, or other man-made chemical additives. If the problem isn't what's in your food, then you have to consider the possibility that you are actually having an immune response to the food itself. There is no 100% accurate way for testing for food sensitivities that I am aware of. They are all capable of yielding false positives and false negatives. What you do have on your side is your intuition. Upon close investigation, most people know the food that is causing the problem. And if you don't know, look at what food or foods you don't want to give up.

"OMG! I can't have ice cream!"

"OMG! How can I live without bread?"

"OMG! I can't eat corn chips!"

"OMG! I'm a vegetarian. If I can't eat soy burgers, where will I get my protein?"

I've heard all of these exclamations, and then some. Unfortunately, we resist giving up our food sensitivities because we become dependant on these problematic foods.

These are the top four inflammatory foods: dairy, wheat, corn, and soy.

Everyone should try experiencing life without these foods for six weeks and see how they feel, even people who don't register any health problems. These foods are like the static noise on a television—you can't truly see when they are creating unnecessary noise in your body. Removing them will give you an excellent baseline for how your body should move and feel. For anyone who has suffered from digestive issues, respiratory distress, or skin irritations, it's a chance to answer the question: Who would I be if I weren't sick?

Identify food sensitivities

Your body loves you. It is always working and adapting in your favor. Many of us have unknowingly wound up living with food sensitivities for years. I will use myself as an example.

I came into the world with ten fingers and ten toes and was declared a healthy baby. My mom breastfed me for about six weeks, then switched me to formula, at which point I developed awful diaper rashes and general skin rashes, and suffered from too many ear infections to count. All were signs of a dairy sensitivity, but we didn't know this at the time.

I grew. Time passed and the rashes went away—kind of. I always had sensitive skin. At age 3, I was diagnosed with asthma. The inflammation from the food sensitivity had moved and become more dramatic in its expression. It was as if my vitality said, "You're not listening to me, so I'm going to make you more miserable. Maybe then you'll pay attention."

Nobody talked to me about what I was eating. Nobody. I did not have a single conversation with a medical professional about food for 25 years, despite many visits to many different kinds of doctors. In the meantime, my immune system was fighting to maintain balance. The human body wants to keep things normal, whatever that means for an individual system. That level of inflammation became my normal state, so I craved the very food that was harming me.

Like an alcoholic or a drug user, where the body adapts to the substance and needs more of it, the food sensitivity sufferer needs a hit of the food that is causing the inflammation to maintain what it perceives as normal. The voices in my head would rise up: "Damn, some cheesecake sounds good." I'd eat it and immediately feel better. So dairy became my favorite food. It can be a vicious cycle until you identify it and do the work to understand and manage it.

I want to say that a lot of people think that the symptoms of food sensitivities are immediate and uncomfortable. While this can be true some of the time, often it's not, especially if you have been consuming the food for decades. Many times the reaction is delayed for days, or maybe you have gotten so used to it that you don't even notice it anymore.

One pattern to look for is what I call "chronic blushing." This syndrome is a red, flushed face along with cold hands and feet. If the digestive tract is hot from an immune response, the blood moves to the core of your body, away from your hands and feet, and heat then rises to your head.

You may also look for chronic musculoskeletal, digestive, skin, and nervous system complaints. This may look like, "I have arthritis. I'm constipated and depressed and I have this annoying patch of eczema on my arm," or "I have acne. My bowel movements are frequent and loose. I feel anxious and my muscles are sore."

What happens when you're not 100% compliant

Early in my healing journey, one of my colleagues asked me to join her for a three-week cleanse, so I removed all four of these inflammatory foods from my diet for three weeks. It wasn't fun. I had a constantly vacuous feeling in my stomach. I'd eat and feel empty. My body would want more food, but I wasn't hungry—except for the very things I was trying to avoid. And this wasn't the more mental phenomenon that can happen with dieting, where you restrict your food choices and then want what you can't have. This was very physiological.

I wasn't yet knowledgeable enough to realize that I hadn't fully removed dairy from my diet. The cleanse involved making smoothies with a high-quality vegetable powder and whey. While whey is free of casein, one of the major allergens in dairy, there are other proteins present that can cause problems.

My elimination diet didn't really work because it wasn't a complete elimination. Yes, I did notice improvements in my well-being and digestion. As a result of this experience, I was also able to fine-tune my normal diet, but I was still wheezing.

Change is a form of loss

So the years pass by and I'm eating the highest quality foods I can get my hands on—sprouted grains, raw dairy, soaked nuts, grass-fed meats, eggs from chickens raised on pasture. You get the drift. Yet I'm still wheezing and inflamed.

A weird bowel pattern shows up where I have a normal bowel movement in the morning, eat breakfast, and then poop 3–5 times after that. Irritating poops, not pleasant at all.

My herbalist at the time said, "Sounds like gluten."

I removed all the grains, not just wheat and corn, from my diet, and my digestion was restored. If you recall, my first attempt at an elimination diet didn't work, but this time it did. Why? Time gave me strength and awareness. Healing is like untangling a wind chime. I share this because we want things to happen fast, and if a dietary intervention or some other natural therapy doesn't work the first time, we too often throw in the towel.

Unfortunately, I was still wheezing, and I'm not talking about mild wheezing. Sometimes I used my Albuterol inhaler hourly.

The years went by, and I attended a nutrition seminar. The teacher started telling his story, which was also my story. He talked about how he had suffered as a child from severe eczema. Asthma is eczema of the lungs; eczema is asthma of the skin. He continued to say that dairy sensitivity is at the root cause of all of it. The body's immune response to dairy often shows up in the epithelial tissue.

I sunk down in my chair, excited and sad at the same time, as I realized that I needed to tell dairy good-bye.

So I made a ceremonial quiche. I lit a candle. Over the span of a few days I savored the quiche, and with the last slice said, "Some day, we may meet again, dairy, but I'm not sure. All I know is that right now, I must bid you farewell. You have brought me much joy over the years, and I thank you for all of the wonderful times, but I think I have outgrown our friendship. Until we meet again ... or not." And I threw dairy a big kiss.

With that dietary intervention and the help of nutritional and herbal lung support, I healed. I am no longer an asthmatic. My skin is nice and smooth. I'm not sick all the time. I live a vital life. I don't need an inhaler to breathe.

Harnessing the power of the five stages of grief

At the time, I didn't realize how important my ceremony with the quiche was until I read more about Elizabeth Kubler-Ross's five stages of grieving:

1. Denial
2. Anger
3. Bargaining
4. Depression
5. Acceptance

Denial looks like this when giving up foods:

When I was 16 years old, my swim coach told me I had a problem with sugar. I said, "No, I don't, but it sounds like you do!" Then, I jumped back in the pool. That's denial.

Anger looks like this when giving up foods:

"Why me?"

"This isn't fair!"

"How could this have happened?"

Yep, I went through this phase. I threw stuff. I screamed at the people I love. I was mad. I went on long walks. I let the anger move through me.

Bargaining looks like this when giving up foods:

"Well, I will just have a little bit of ice cream every now and then."

"Not now. Maybe later."

"I will just keep putting cream in my coffee. Is that ok?"

Bargaining is an attempt to avoid the grief.

I bargained with my food sensitivities for years. Following my hospitalization when my health had collapsed, it took me four years to give up gluten and another three to give up dairy. I just kept bargaining, until it hurt too much. I had to change.

Depression looks like this when giving up foods:

"This sucks, I'm not sure it's worth it. Why bother?"

"I can't go out with my friends for dinner. They are going to order a dessert that I can't eat! I will just stay home."

"Life's just not worth living without these foods."

Yep, I lost more than foods when I gave up gluten and dairy. I lost friends, too. I had a circle of friends who would binge on dessert (i.e., eat a whole cookie-cake with icing all over it) and then go run it off. Those friendships didn't last. I wallowed in despair for quite some time, but it wasn't pathological depression. It was a healthy process of letting go.

Acceptance looks like this when giving up foods:
"I think I feel some hope for the future."
"I'm ready. I can do this. It's going to be ok."
Damn straight, it's ok. It's more than ok. It is the beginning of your new life—free of inflammatory foods and all of the unnecessary drama that they entail.

If you can hear your body whisper, you won't have to listen to it scream.

I share my story with you because life is in the details. Healing begins with the ability to observe yourself. This is at the core of consciousness.

You are not your thoughts. You are the observer of your thoughts.

You are not your body. You are the observer of your body.

What is it trying to communicate to you? Are you listening?

If you can't be an objective observer, find a professional, someone who can witness your body and your life, and teach *you* how to be an observer.

All in all, it took me four years to figure out I had a problem with gluten and another three to find out that dairy was an even more severe sensitivity. After years of antibiotics, corticosteroids, sugar, and sleep deprivation, it took a while for my vitality to unwind and express itself.

Wherever you are on your healing journey, start with small changes and let life show itself from there. There are hundreds, thousands, millions of people diagnosed with chronic diseases that are just cover-up labels for the real causes of the problem: poor diet and lifestyle habits. Take responsibility for your life and examine what you put into your mouth and how your body responds. The answers you are seeking are there—in your body. Give it time and hone your observational skills.

Beyond food sensitivities

Obviously, food sensitivities are not at the root of every digestive disturbance. The digestive tract is complex. It is at the core of your very being. Stress, for example, diverts all of the energy from digestion into your arms and legs. There's no energy to digest food when there is an emergency and you need to be prepared to fight and run.

If you cannot digest your food well, then you cannot digest life well. And if you stop and think about it, the brain actually looks like smushed up intestines! The title of Dr. Michael Gershon's book, *The Second Brain*, really says it all. The entire book is about serotonin, a feel-good neurotransmitter in your brain that is produced in the gut.

And you thought you were in charge?

Your digestive system is your immune system. One of

my teachers, the late Dr. Michael Dobbins, used to say that the immune system is a portable digestive system.

That is so interesting. Think about it.

What you eat represents the largest benefit or threat to your well-being. Your digestive tract asks questions: What is that? Is it a friend? Do I let it in? Is it a problem? Do I excrete it? That is exactly what your immune system does. I think of the immune system as literally floating around the body performing a digestive function.

Your digestive system is your immune system.

Your immune system is your digestive system.

The interconnection of all things in this world is right here in your body, particularly when it comes to your microbiome, which exhibits both digestive and immune functions. The microbiome refers to all of the microorganisms living in and on specific areas of your body. There are more of these microorganisms than there are human cells that make up your body. Yes, human cells are larger, but the microorganisms we can't see greatly outnumber us, and here's the scoop: they were here long before you were. These microorganisms are ancient and when we kiss, hug, give birth, breastfeed, or make love, we exchange them. If that's not a lesson in the Oneness, then I don't know what is!

So, it would make sense that eating something your body doesn't evolutionarily recognize, or taking an unnecessary round of antibiotics that disrupts the diversity of your microorganisms, creates confusion in your being's core.

How to specifically support the microbiome is beyond

the scope of this book, but I will say that this is why probiotics (bacteria), prebiotics (food for the bacteria), and fermented foods are so important. They nourish this aspect of our bodies and remind us that our systems are far from sterile.

In the chapter Heal in Peace I will discuss how we get sick. Here is a teaser: it is rarely about the pathogen. Sure, there are some strong viruses and bacteria that can overcome a healthy body, but more often than not, the tissue is unhealthy and has become a welcoming home to a particular disease-causing microbe. A portable digestive system would come in quite handy, yes? Something that could clean up the tissues and restore vitality?

You do not have an immune system. You are an immune system.

The specialization in different branches of medicine is literally killing us. You cannot separate the body into neat little compartments. The mucus membranes, where the immune system resides, talk to each other and provide a home to beneficial (and potentially harmful) microorganisms. If there is a problem in the digestive tract, a very large mucus membrane with a surface area the size of a studio apartment, then that could reflect back to other mucus membranes. In my case, my digestive tract inflammation reflected back to my lungs. But the inflammation in your digestive tract could also show up in your sinus cavity, eyes, gall bladder, or even vaginal tissue. These are all mucus membranes.

The inflammation can even move to the brain and cause seizures. That's right. A food sensitivity that starts as a diaper rash on a baby can move into the nervous system as the child grows. There is one case study involving a man who discovered his dairy sensitivity was the underlying cause of his congestive heart failure.[5]

Leave no stone unturned. Leave no food unexamined.

Doesn't this information make you want to listen to your body in a new way?

Bitter makes it better.

One of the solutions to healthy digestion is the bitter taste. There are now six recognized tastes in foods: bitter, sweet, salty, sour, pungent, and umami (a Japanese word for savory or overall deliciousness). Some would argue that bland and astringent are also tastes. That's ok, too. The more the merrier.

What I want you to understand is that the bitter taste is really what distinguishes food from herbs. This taste has been removed from our food supply. Farming has literally bred it out of plants. "Ewwww!" we exclaim, as our faces contort. "That's so bitter! I don't like it!"

But life isn't all about pleasure. Not everything is sweet. Living well involves accepting discomfort.

The pain of an acute infection.

The pain of childbirth.

The pain of grieving.

The pain of physical exertion.

Discomfort is transformational. "No pain, no gain" is a real phenomenon, if you use your discomfort to expand your consciousness.

Bitter is the taste of vitality.

Bitter is a primal experience of being human.

Bitter enlivens you.

Not everything you eat needs to taste good. Herbs are medicine.

You may not like it initially, but your body will begin to LOVE it. Then you will start to crave it and your diet just won't feel complete without it.

Proof

In 2009, I set up an herb bar at one of our continuing education seminars. All types of holistic health professionals join us there regularly to learn about whole food nutrition and herbal medicine. I served two herbal tonics—an energy tonic and a brain tonic. A few attendees were excited, but not many. Most came up to the bar, took a dose, grimaced, and walked away.

Despite all the negative feedback, I kept educating at our events and within our community of health professionals. I kept passing out samples, urging people to listen to their bodies, practically screaming, "Your body will love you for this! Give it enough time—you will crave this taste that you despise!"

(I decided long ago that since plants can't talk, I would talk for them.)

Over months and then years, the herb bar expanded. I went from serving two tonics to a dozen. There are now so many people at the herb bar during seminar breaks that we had to purchase large dispensers.

Here are some of the comments I've heard from people on Sunday mornings, after three doses of herbs on Saturday:

> "I know this sounds really weird, but when I woke up this morning, the texture of my skin had changed. It is softer and clearer. It is subtle but the change is there!"

> "I hate going to the grocery store, but yesterday, on my way home, going to the grocery store was effortless. I just pulled in, parked my car, and it was no big deal. It's the herbs. I just feel different in a good way."

> "I'm usually exhausted at the end of an all-day seminar, but last night, I went home and I wanted to cook dinner. That never happens! I wanted to be with my family!"

> "When I came to the seminar yesterday, I had a headache. In the past, it would just get worse as the day went on, but it went away. I felt it coming, but it just went away."

"You know how you have those things that you can never get to? Well, my thing is cleaning out this drawer in my kitchen that is just full of crap. I got home and just did it! No problem. Done."

"I haven't pooped in four days. Within minutes of taking a dose of the herbs, I went to the bathroom. So cool!"

"You wouldn't guess it by looking at me, but I am highly anxious. It's, like, inside my body, I just feel so tight. After just a single dose, something in me calmed down. I can't believe it."

I want to be clear that the brain and energy tonics also provide support to the nervous system, hormones, and immune system, which accounts for these positive experiences. This goes far beyond the effects of bitters as a classification of herbs to aid digestion. But they are all still inherently bitter.

Incorporate this taste into your life, and Nature will reward you with better digestion, clearer thinking, and more energy.

The bitter taste gets you out of your head and into your body like nothing else can. That is its essence. The bitter taste pulls your energy down and into your core, enhancing digestion along every step of the way.

Bitters immediately turn on your digestive function, including appetite regulation. Whether someone under- or overeats, bitters can help. They cause the hydrochloric acid to increase in your stomach, which aids protein digestion and appropriate peristalsis (the rhythmic motion of smooth muscle in your digestive tract). If the bowels move too fast, you get diarrhea and cramping. If they move too slowly you get constipated. In the digestive tract, a problem downstream is usually caused by a problem upstream. Bitters address the problem upstream.

Another effect after taking a bitter herb is that pancreatic function improves. The positive effects here are twofold. You will be rewarded with the appropriate release of insulin, which supports blood sugar regulation, and you will enjoy better digestive enzyme production, which helps break down starches.

Liver and gall bladder function improve. Bitters exhibit choleretic and cholagogue activity. This is a fancy way of saying that the bitter taste results in improved bile production and bile flow.

Why should you care about your bile? Bile is your body's natural laxative. It acts as an irritant to the digestive lining and also carries out waste products. You want your bile to move. Stagnant bile is toxic.

Bitters turn on your digestive fire. Just as fire is transformational, turning wood into light and then ash, your digestion turns food into fuel, building blocks for your body, and then poop.

Most importantly, bitters ignite the fire of intuitive eating. As this taste weaves its way into your life, you will feel more connected to your body. There is wisdom in your body that lies dormant until this taste returns.

When I take my herbal medicine, I say a silent prayer to the plants: "Please teach me what foods are good for my body. Infinite Spirit, show me the way." Bitters fine-tune your relationship to Nature and to yourself, drawing you deeper into your unique way of being, building trust and bringing forth the unique you.

Bitter is the new sweet.

As Dr. Robert Lustig, who specializes in childhood obesity, explains regarding the cause of our obesity epidemic: "Nature made sugar hard to get; man made it easy."[6] Bitters, however, can help us ease our dependence on sugar.

Sugar is a drug. It lights up the addictive part of the brain more than cocaine. Sometimes the answer to addiction is not removing the substance from your life, but asking the question: what is missing from your life?

The answer to easing our addiction to sugar and refined carbohydrates is not necessarily going cold turkey, but instead adding the bitter taste.

Bitter deficiency syndrome is a real concern.

As James Green explains in his book *The Male Herbal*:

"It is my opinion that the nearly complete lack of bitter flavored foods in the overall U.S. and Canadian diet is a major contributing factor to common cultural health imbalances such as PMS, . . . other female and male reproductive-organ difficulties, hormonal imbalances, migraine headaches, indigestion, liver and gall bladder dysfunction, abnormal metabolism, hypoglycemia, and diabetes."[7]

In other words, it's not all about digestion. Bitter herbs enhance immune function in the sinuses, skin, and lungs, and improve white blood-cell function. They boost physical performance and act as a general tonic to improve overall health. They exhibit anti-inflammatory and anti-allergic activity, and appear to have an effect on mucus production and how it moves in the sinuses and lungs.

How is all of this possible, you ask? Well, science is discovering bitter taste receptors all over the body, including the brain and testes.[8]

So suck it up, buttercup! You need this taste in your life.

We need more than the bitter taste of chocolate, coffee, and beer made with hops. The more you want to cover up the bitter tastes in these foods with sugar and the more you cringe at the thought of the bitter taste, the more you need it. Educate your taste buds with bitters, and soon that ice cream you eat will taste a little too sweet, and those artificial little candies you can't resist will taste downright yucky.

My three favorite bitter remedies

1. Dandelion root—Taraxacum officinale

Most people curse this herb as an annoying weed. But the fact that this plant grows out of sidewalks teaches us something: it is strong and resilient. We benefit from consuming these hardy types of plants. It's almost like it irritates us on purpose, saying, "Hey! Look at me! I'm right here! Pay attention! You need me to be healthy in this modern world!"

Dandelion is the perfect illustration of Nature's wisdom. The leaves support the kidneys, while the roots support the liver. You can't talk about liver function without talking about kidney function. These organs dance together: if one is struggling, the other will compensate. Dandelion is the perfect DJ to get these two organs moving in sync.

On the sweet side of bitters, dandelion is a very gentle liver remedy. It is very earthy in its flavor, kind of like a root vegetable with a bit more kick. Try it in herbal coffee substitutes, like Dandy Blend and Reishi Roast, to give you a more specific idea of how it tastes. It is a great daily tonic to support healthy bile production and flow, and exhibits cleansing qualities.

2. Globe artichoke leaf—Cynara scolymus

Most people are familiar with artichoke as a food. What we usually eat is the bract. The medicine we are discussing here is the leaf. It's bitter. Bitter. Bitter. With . . . a hint of popcorn.

Not only does globe artichoke leaf offer the bitter effect, but it also profoundly protects the liver. Think of this herb when someone is not willing to give up his or her vices, like, "I know I need to stop eating fried foods, but I can't," or "I really want to quit smoking, but not yet," or "Yes, I probably have one too many glasses of wine before dinner, but I just don't want to go there right now."

It is also an awesome plant to address what is known

as a diagnosis of exclusion. This happens when the medical system is unable to find a cause for a person's discomfort, so their condition gets a vague label like "irritable bowel syndrome" or "stomach upset."

One client came to me after having suffered from nausea for two years with little to no relief. She had been through numerous diagnostic procedures, revealing no answers. She was painfully living in a mystery. At the end of our session, she mentioned that she was a recovered alcoholic, and I thought, "BINGO!" Maybe, just maybe, a little liver support would help after years of stressing it with drinking.

I put together a globe artichoke leaf and peppermint leaf tea for her, since peppermint also offers digestive support and mitigates some of the bitter taste of globe artichoke. She took it home, and within hours called me to report that her nausea was finally subsiding. She finished the bag of tea and her complaints did not return.

Is globe artichoke the answer to everything that ails you? Of course not. But the story illustrates what is possible to achieve with medicinal tools and tastes that are often missing from our modern lifestyles.

3. Gentian root—Gentiana lutea

Gentian root is a straight bitter. If you recall, dandelion root is on the sweet side of bitter, and globe artichoke is bitter with a hint of popcorn, which indicates the presence of a touch of aromatics. Not so much with gentian. Gentian is simply bitter.

Gentian is extremely helpful to weary people who have lost their appetite for food (and life). These people may also suffer from functional digestive complaints, like gas, cramping, constipation, general stomach upset, and maybe even depression. Gentian stimulates, so it is great for those people who may complain of a sense of heaviness or sluggishness in their bodies or digestive tracts.

Gentian also combines well with other bitter herbs. Sometimes after a rough day, when I get home and start dinner, I'll feel tension in my abdomen, like it's not ready for dinner. I'll put a half teaspoon of globe artichoke extract and a quarter teaspoon of gentian in a wine glass, and fill it with sparkling water. It's almost like drinking a beer. It tastes divine and immediately shifts my digestion. I always eat well after a tonic made with these herbs.

I also find that I sleep well, too, because the herbs turn on my parasympathetic (peaceful) nervous system. Which leads us to the next important part of living in peace: getting enough rest.

CHAPTER 5

REST IN PEACE

"Every other creature on the face of the earth seems to know how to be quiet and still. A butterfly on a leaf, a cat in front of a fireplace, even a hummingbird comes to rest sometime. But humans are constantly on the go. We seem to have lost the ability to just be quiet, to simply be present in the stillness that is the foundation of our lives. Yet if we never get in touch with that stillness, we never fully experience our lives."

—JOHN DAIDO LOORI

A side from death, sleeping is the ultimate stillness. If you stop and think about it, going to bed each night is a little bit like dying, and waking up each morning is a little like being born.

This perspective gives new meaning and respect to your sleep and waking cycles, doesn't it?

It makes sleeping a spiritual experience of letting go.

Sleeping well requires that you feel safe in the world. The minute I start ruminating about a situation or a problem, trying to figure out what I did or said that was wrong, analyzing another's behavior, or what I wish I had said, the quality of my sleep goes down the tubes.

The 12-step program for healing addictions states, "Let go and let God." What a great phrase to carry with you into dreamland.

When we forget that we are not in control, we work too much. Corporations, along with the medical system, treat the human frame like it is a machine. Our modern systems ask too much from us.

Work more.

Plan more.

Read more,

Make more money.

Organize more.

You are not enough.

Entire industries exist that entice us with MORE.

Nature doesn't work like that. Nature cycles.

In the spring, the leaves are a translucent green. Fresh. Almost wet. The energy in the plants is moving upwards, fully expressing itself.

In the summer, the leaves turn a darker green. We enjoy fruits and berries, and slowly plants start to dry out from the heat.

The late summer is the season for harvest, storing our food for the winter.

In autumn, the leaves turn brown and fall from the trees. The energy in the plant moves down into the roots. No more green leaves and no more fruit.

In the winter, all is quiet and brown—white with snow, if you're lucky. Most plant life is dead or dormant.

We are supposed to participate in these cycles.

Nothing grows all the time. Each day, and each activity you participate in, has a cycle. There are limiting factors in Nature, which you are a part of, whether or not you know it.

You have to consciously decide when enough is enough. Take your life back. Aim for quality, not quantity.

Quality sleep.

Quality food.

Quality time.

On our last family vacation, I sat on the beach a lot with my son Drake. When I wasn't helping him build sandcastles, I made my own designs in the sand and just watched Nature at work.

In late afternoon, the sun gradually softened and the breeze got cooler and the colors shifted in the sky. I realized that Nature does an extraordinary job of easing us into the "dark time," as my son calls it. The sun goes down gently, not suddenly. The colors soften in the span of hours, not minutes.

We miss these subtleties in our modern world. We want to go-go-go all day long. When it's dark, turn on a light.

Send off that last e-mail.

Do a load of laundry.

Finish that project.

All after the sun goes down.

Then, we lie in our beds and can't sleep. No shit. This is not a surprise. The nervous system doesn't work like that. It doesn't have an on/off switch. It requires cues. You need to invite sleep.

A good dinner.

A hot bath.

A cup of tea.

Candles.

Some calming herbs.

Good conversation with family members that brings closure to your day.

Keep your life simple after the sun goes down. Your nervous system will thank you with better sleep.

Reclaim your day of rest

When did Sunday stop being a day of rest and start being a day of catch-up? I remember when stores used to close on Sunday. Now, almost everything is open.

I am a huge fan of what I call a pajama day. A friend of mine calls it her no-car day. Whatever you want to name it, Sunday used to be a day of rest, but for many it's not anymore.

If we want something different in our lives, we have to create it. Lack of rest in our culture contributes to inflammatory chronic disease states, mental illness, stress, and more.

It's not just enough to sleep well. We have to learn how to move more slowly and more mindfully.

What continues to amaze me is that I can check ten things off my to-do list, but my mind will focus on the five things I didn't get done. Now, I try to be aware of this as often as possible. When my mind wanders in that direction, I just say, "Ok, but don't forget all the things you did do!"

Take a deep breath

All that stuff you think you have to do today can wait. It's not going anywhere. You're not a better person for working 14-hour days and sleeping five hours a night; you're foolish. I know, because I used to be one of those people—and if I'm not careful, I will be again.

The world has become a vortex for busy-ness. It is so easy to get sucked into it all. It becomes a daily practice to sidestep this chaotic frenzy.

Let this be your reminder to take a few minutes—or even hours—to yourself today and find a way to rest, even if you lie down with your eyes wide open.

Your liver wants you to lie down.

That tired feeling at the end of the day is a build-up of metabolic waste products. All day long your liver is receiving blood from the portal circulation, blood coming up from the lower bowels. It works against gravity until you lie down, at which point the blood pools in the liver. Then, the liver cleans the blood very efficiently and you wake up refreshed.

Or not.

Sometimes if this cycle is incomplete and you don't get enough rest, you will wake up with a frontal headache and feel like you have a hangover, when you didn't party at all. Sometimes eating before bed will do this. Your body has better things to do than digest your food during sleep! Ideally, your last meal would be three hours before bedtime.

This also points to the wisdom of an afternoon siesta. When I lie down with my toddler in the afternoon, I may not sleep but I will lie down, and I feel better for it because my liver gets a break.

News flash: while you're resting, your body is working.

A lot of people think that they've got better things to do than sleep, inferring that sleep is akin to doing nothing. Sleep creates you, just like food does.

Don't compromise it.

Self-mastery begins with food and ends with sleep.

Ever notice that after a bad night's sleep you're hungry all day, specifically for carbohydrates?

That is a real phenomenon created by your hormones. Don't ever forget how smart your body is. If it doesn't get energy from restorative sleep, then it will get it from different forms of sugar, which will rev you up, creating a vicious cycle where you can't sleep and then you . . . Need. More. Sugar.

This insight is based on the Chinese Medicine Meridian Clock, which represents thousands of years of collected wisdom. The closer to 9 p.m. that you go to sleep, the more restorative your sleep will be. Going to bed at midnight and sleeping in won't make you feel as alive. Going to bed between 9 and 11 p.m. restores your endocrine system, which includes your capacity to regulate your blood sugar.

Traditional Chinese Medicine recognizes that your chi or life force dives down to restore specific tissues at specific times. Pay attention to when you wake up in the middle of the night, particularly if it is a repetitive experience. You might learn something about yourself. Below are the hours of organ regeneration, according to the Chinese Medicine Meridian Clock:

7–9 p.m. Sex Organs/Circulation

9–11 p.m. Thyroid/Adrenal

11 p.m.–1 a.m. Gall bladder

1–3 a.m. Liver

3–5 a.m. Lungs

5–7a.m. Large intestine

7–9 a.m. Stomach

When my asthma was really bad, I would wake up between 3 and 5 a.m. to use my inhaler. That makes sense now!

It can be hard, I mean, really, really hard, to get to bed close to 9 p.m. Discipline is defined as the ability to follow your own commands. Going to bed early enough requires all the discipline you can muster.

Years ago, when I was living in a basement apartment in McLean, Virginia, my life felt completely out of control, and I was struggling, grasping at straws. My therapist asked me one simple question, "Well, Charlotte, what can you control that would be good for you?" My immediate response was: my bedtime.

For one full week, I made a commitment to sleep with the sun. It was summer time, so it wasn't unrealistic, like it might be in the winter. When the sun went down around 8:30, I was in bed and asleep by 9, and I woke up with the birds around 5:30 and was out of bed before 6:00.

I felt like a rock star.

Many people have this experience when camping. It was not sustainable for me to live this way, but it gave me a chance to experience how much difference such a rhythm could make. Every now and then I return to this sleep cycle to deeply restore my energy and vitality.

Then again, maybe disrupted sleeping patterns are normal.

One of the most interesting theories on sleep comes from Carol Worthman, an anthropologist. She proposes that our sleeping patterns shift throughout our lives because we used to sleep in groups, wiring people to be wakeful at different stages in their life.

Teenagers like to stay up late and then sleep in.

Elders often fall asleep early, only to discover that they can only sleep for three to four hours at a time.

Middle-aged adults can go either way.

In *Dreamland: Adventures in the Strange Science of Sleep*, David K. Randall comments, "These overlapping shifts could be a way to ensure that someone in the family is always awake and keeping watch, or at least close to it. In this ancient system, it makes sense that older adults who are unable to move as fast as the rest of the family are naturally jumpy, never staying in deep sleep for long, simply because they were the most vulnerable to the unknown".[9]

Not only does this theory make good sense, but it also facilitates acceptance. We all know what it feels like to lie down at night knowing we're not going to sleep because it's too early, or because we anticipate jolting awake at 2 a.m. and not getting back to sleep until right before the alarm goes off. It's a unique form of torture to lie there fighting your body and mind, trying to convince yourself to sleep. But what if we just accepted that we're supposed to be awake at that hour? Wouldn't that be more relaxing?

Especially if we keep thinking that something is wrong. This theory may allow some to relax into their sleep dys-regulation, embracing restful wakefulness.

It's not all about sleep

Sometimes sleep isn't enough.

Sometimes you need a break from your life.

This is the rest that comes from a vacation, preferably spent in nature. We need to create distance from our lives so that we can begin to see them as they really are. In our daily lives, we cannot see what we are caught up in. A vacation is a way to step outside of that so you can become an observer of yourself.

The weekly pajama day can help, but do what you can to get more rest.

Let me assure you that I am well aware that we have major socioeconomic inequalities in this country. Not everyone can take naps. Not everyone can take a vacation. Some people work at night and sleep during the day. I don't have any answers, only the suggestion that you do what you can with what you have, and resist being a victim of the system.

A few words to parents

The sleep deprivation that comes with parenting a baby or young child is real and extremely difficult.

Every child is different.

Every parent is different.

Every family is different.

There is no one solution to sleeping well, eating well, or living well. And life-altering events like pregnancy and childcare can throw our few self-imposed rules out the window.

I can get so frustrated when it seems my only quiet time is at 8:30 at night, when I'm tired but long for an uninterrupted conversation with my husband, or something fun like a movie. The early years of parenting are difficult to navigate and require constant negotiation.

Sleep deprivation in the early months and years of your child's life is a humbling experience that can bring you to your knees. But consider, for a moment, that the divine design of pregnancy and parenting might make you helpless for a very good reason. New parenthood is a sacred time. You have just brought new life into this world, and you can't do it all. You need to ask for help. Since Drake was born, my mother has become an integral part of our lives, and we are fortunate to have hired help in our house when we need it.

You must find a way to create your very own village so that you can get the rest you need.

In the meantime, don't try to escape the pain of parenting. When I was a new parent I was commiserating with a friend, who said, "We just did whatever made life easier." Ok, I thought. Easy isn't always right. Most shortcuts have negative consequences long-term. For example, letting our baby "cry it out" so that we could sleep did not work for us.

This sleep training technique encourages learned helplessness, which ignites the stress response in a baby. Instead, our son slept with us.

Sleep deprivation associated with parenting is another example of a good pain. Embrace the challenge, and it will stretch you in unimaginable ways.

Maturity comes from perseverance in both you and your child.

A few words to pet owners

Please, oh please, get your pets out of your bedroom. Having a dog or cat in your bed is like sleeping with a child who will never grow up. Pets do affect the quality of your sleep, particularly if they are on top of your head! But the real problem, particularly if you suffer from allergies, is that a pet can be what naturopathic medicine calls an "obstacle to cure." Many people are allergic to their pet's hair, and since the animals are close to the ground, they also carry pollen, mold, and dust on their bodies.

I had to give up my dog.

I know what it's like to walk away from love for the sake of health.

It was hard.

But it was worth it. The pay-off was huge.

While getting a pet out of your bed (or in some cases, on to a happy life with someone new) may be a big decision, vitality is more a result of hundreds of little decisions you make during the day, such as whether to sleep in an extra half hour or get out of bed for a morning walk. So far we have looked at what to eat and drink, how to support healthy digestion, and when to go to bed. Now, we will move on to one of my favorites: exercise.

CHAPTER 6

MOVE IN PEACE

"For the past ten years, I've been slowly killing myself.
Weapon of choice?
Kale and running shoes."

—SARAH ROMERO

The opposite of rest is movement. The combination of not enough sleep and too much exercising, in the presence of nutritional deficiencies, is often the straw that breaks the camel's back. It compromises repair mechanisms in the body and can put you into a chronic state of inflammation, where sleep can't relieve your fatigue.

Fitness is not the same as wellness, but once again we often collapse the meanings of these two words.

We see fit people and think, "Damn, I wish I were that healthy," when in fact, often they aren't! I can honestly say that when I was fittest, I was also my unhealthiest.

When it comes to wellness, exercise needs to be enjoyable and in the Goldilocks zone: not too much, not too little—ohhh, that's just right.

We live in a culture of more, more, more, especially with sports. I became a victim to it at an early age. I started swimming competitively when I was 7 years old, continued through college, and then in my early twenties, started competing in triathlons. I was always tired and never fully recovered from my workouts. I considered this a badge of honor.

In fact, when I was in college, I didn't have my menstrual cycle for 3 years. At first I was concerned, but when I went to the doctor, he said, "Oh yeah. You're a healthy woman. We see this all the time in female athletes with low body fat. Here's a sample of birth control pills and here's your prescription. That'll fix you up nicely. Have a good day." So I walked out of his office with my package of pills, unaware there was, in fact, a deeper problem.

Back at the pool, my coach would say, "Hey, Charlotte! You're looking so fit and lean! Keep up the good work!"

Women need body fat for healthy hormone production. Can you be a healthy female athlete? Maybe. I suppose I am biased, because for the female athletes who come to see me, clearly something's not working.

Case in point: I had a client who said, "You know, something strange is happening. I injured my knee a few weeks ago and can't run, so I started going to yoga class, and I've lost 5 pounds. I can't make sense of it."

YES!

I tried to make the most of the teaching moment with her. I explained that for some people, cardiovascular activity ignites the stress response, which increases inflammation, and the resulting hormonal imbalance actually makes it harder to lose weight. Prolonged stress contributes to high cortisol, which contributes to weight gain. But just like me many years ago, she didn't get it, and as soon as her knee healed, she went right back to her cardiovascular exercise and straight back into her stressed-induced, inflammatory cascade from hell.

Another client, who was exercising 3 hours a day to control his blood sugar, went on vacation. To his surprise, his blood sugar came down into the normal range. Once again, cortisol, as a part of the stress response, raises blood sugar. Yet he felt guilty for not sticking to his exercise routine, and as soon as he got home, he resumed his exercise regimen. His blood sugar immediately went back up. Did he stop? Not at all.

Please, we have to stop living in our heads and get into our bodies.

We think more exercise is better for us, just like we think that a low-fat diet is better for us, and we suffer.

Professional athletes are an anomaly. Their bodies have particular attributes, which help them to participate in specific sports. For example, basketball players are often unusually tall, swimmers generally have very long torsos, and baseball players often have extraordinary eyesight.

The message that you can do anything, so beloved by our society, is not true.

So is the idea that you can exercise or eat your way to the perfect body of your dreams. It is such bullshit.

Exercise is like perfection. It can be very destructive while disguising itself as a noble pursuit. I exercised because I thought it was good for me. In doing so, I did not respect my body's limits, and I damaged my health.

Even after my vitality collapsed, I continued to exercise like a maniac, as my mother would say. In that cycle, exercising excessively had become my only way to feel alive. The real reason I did so, however, was that I had a pattern of disordered eating, bingeing on my food sensitivities and sugar and then "running it off." If you find yourself in this cycle, please know it's not your fault, but it is your responsibility to change. These patterns are not sustainable and can damage your body.

Exercising for vitality

Let's say you are on the other end of the spectrum: a couch potato. My message to you is the same: find your happy medium. You don't have to exercise yourself into misery, just like you don't have to diet yourself into misery.

Chinese Medicine states that stagnation is the cause of a hundred diseases. Our bodies must move or the blood and the breath get stuck, and we get sick.

Here's all you have to do to exercise in a way that promotes health:

Get outside. When I say exercise, most people conjure up an image of a gym. No wonder they don't want to do it!

Can you feel the difference in your body between swimming in a pool and swimming in a lake or the ocean?

Can you feel the difference between walking on a treadmill and walking in the woods with the rocks underneath your feet and the sounds of the trees?

Can you feel the difference between riding a stationary bike and riding down the road with the sun on your skin and the wind in your hair?

Nature humbles us. It puts us in our place, as guests in someone else's house.

Exercising on machines says, "I am in control of my destiny. You don't own me, Stairmaster! I own you!" Exercise machines can also say the opposite: "You can't trust your body! Program me to push you and then I will wow you with the numbers of calories you just burned." Either way, the human being is robbed of vitality, as you give away your personal power to a machine, instead of listening to your body and moving it out of enjoyment.

To me, it doesn't get any better than a nice walk outside. It doesn't matter if you like the weather. A walk outside, no matter how cold, hot, or wet, is healing. You don't have to enjoy it, just do it! According to Richard Louv, author of *Last Child in the Woods* and *The Nature Principle*, researchers have measured that being outside has positive effects on people's health, even when they're uncomfortable: "memory performance and attention spans improved 20 percent after just an hour of interacting with nature."[10]

Our bodies not only need to move, they must move! The best thing to do is experiment with different forms of movement to see what feels right to you. Just like eating, exercise should always make you feel good. Your feeling of wellness, not how many calories you burn, is your barometer for success.

Many people need restorative movement, not excessive cardiovascular activity. Restorative movement includes: restorative yoga, tai chi, chi gong, rebounding, swimming, and of course, walking. This was very difficult for me to accept during my healing process because I was so used to pushing myself.

Everyone moves in peace and eats in peace differently. In each case, you need to listen to your body and respect your unique needs. It's just like food. It all has a place, but you have to consider what is most appropriate for YOU.

Running is hugely popular—it's free but for the cost of

a pair of sneakers, and it shows fast results. However, many people injure themselves running.

I have talked to chiropractors who are more concerned about the harms of yoga than of contact sports because they've treated so many women who have pushed themselves too hard in class and hurt their backs.

Do you see what I'm talking about? Nothing is appropriate for everyone, and how you participate in a specific type of exercise matters. You are in charge of your body, not your coach, not your instructor, and not the machine.

Also, just like eating, what works for you is also likely to change throughout your life. Give yourself permission to change activities.

That said, strength training is awesome health insurance.

On the first day of a family vacation, I fell very hard on some rocks, losing my footing and landing in a very contorted way. Our entire time together could have been ruined. Everyone who saw me go down thought, "Here we go to the hospital!" Eek! I sat there. Took some deep breaths. As I checked in with my body, all I had was a lot of scratches and bruises on the top of my foot. Nothing broken. Nothing sprained.

Another time, I was walking in the rain, holding my 8-month-old. I lost my footing on the wet sidewalk and came down hard on my elbow (Fortunately, Drake fell into the grass). I am convinced that my arm should have broken, but it didn't. I had a few bad bruises, and that was that.

Obviously, I will never know whether I was saved from serious injury by the unconscious grace of my body protecting itself, or the good strong body and bones created by my workouts. After my falls, I certainly felt gratitude for both.

I share these stories because if there's one thing I know, it's that weight-bearing exercise is essential to your vitality. I use the Slow Burn or Super Slow technique. It has been a great fit for me. Strong muscles create strong bones, which create a strong person. That physical strength also translates into emotional and mental fortitude. Nothing exists in isolation. When you build muscle, you strengthen your mind, your emotional resiliency, and your overall adaptability. You can't help but take the confidence built with this exercise routine and bring it out into the world. It's a good hurt and a worthy investment in your future vitality, not to mention your present well-being.

This is very different from cardiovascular exercise, which can deplete the body and ignite the stress response. Eating whatever you want and then exercising it off exhausts your endocrine system. No matter what you may think, you can't outrun your fork.

At this point I hope you are starting to see that wellness is a mosaic. There is no one thing, but many moving parts, that lead to vitality. Before we tie it all together, let's examine one more topic: acute infections.

CHAPTER 7

HEAL IN PEACE

"Being sick is not a condemnation or a moral judgment, but a movement in a larger process of healing and restoration."

—KEN WILBUR

This is the most important chapter in this book, especially if you have children. I'm about to encourage you toward the most important paradigm shift you may ever make.

In April of 2002, the medical system failed me for the last time. As I described in the first chapter, I had been sick for over a month, on multiple rounds of antibiotics, and finally admitted to the hospital for possible surgery to remove my gall bladder. Five thousand dollars' worth of tests later, doctors discovered that I had a mononucleosis infection, at which point they cast me aside and said, "Go home, sleep, and drink lots of water."

That's all they could offer me.

It wasn't enough.

Aboriginal healer Kakkib li'Dthia Warrawee'a, in his book *There Once Was a Tree Called Deru*, points out that the "slaughter of the pathogen fails to cure the patient."[11] In other words, you can't kill your way back to health, and getting rid of symptoms doesn't mean getting rid of the illness. A true professional in that hospital could have sat with me and had another conversation. Maybe it simply would have gone something like this:

"Hey, you look and feel like crap. I can see that. But here's what you need to understand: Mono is caused by the Epstein Barr virus. Did you know that 98% of the population carries this virus? And yet not everyone gets acutely ill from it. Why is that? Well, it's about how well you live your life. For some reason, your body became hospitable to this bug. I bet you haven't been sleeping. Maybe you have a stressful job and then you eat lots of sweets to get some energy. Bottom line: you didn't get sick by accident. Let me give you a business card for a naturopath who can teach you about your body and how to care for it so this doesn't happen again."

Sound ridiculous? Maybe. But how wonderful it would be if more doctors asked their patients to tell them about how they're living, not just how they're feeling. The medical establishment needs to measure success by preventing disease, not by treating disease. I want to live in that world.

When I got sick, I was sleeping four hours a night, eating an obscene amount of sugar, exercising excessively, and working a stressful job as manager of a busy restaurant. I didn't really know any better—I just thought that was adulthood. Overcoming illness is rarely about beating the virus or bacteria, but rather about making your vitality so strong that the bugs can't take hold.

Being sick is no fun. It sucks. It hurts. It can be depressing. Sometimes living feels like you're dying, and you are. But it doesn't always mean that there is something wrong... it means that something is right.

Let me explain.

Getting sick is healthy.

Somewhere along the way you had a bad night's sleep, consumed too much sugar, ate the food you're sensitive to, or got into a heated fight with a family member. This created physical and emotional stress that suppressed your immune system, so when a virus, bacterium, or parasite crossed your path, you couldn't fight back and you became sick. Your body entered survival mode and had better things to do than repair damaged tissue, which then become the perfect home for a pathogenic microbe.

Getting sick is a time to reflect on your life. How did I get here? All too often we think the answer to acute illness is to just make it go away.

If you've ever had the flu, you know that it makes you ache so deeply in your bones that your hair and skin hurt. That pain comes from messenger molecules in your immune system called cytokines, which are doing an extraordinary job of getting you well. However, instead of embracing the temporary pain of living in a sick body, we try to escape it with anti-inflammatory drugs.

But that's a mistake.

The inflammation of an acute infection heals the body. If you take an anti-inflammatory drug to minimize the ache or the fever that accompanies acute infection, then you have set yourself up for chronic inflammatory disease, like autoimmune disease and cancer, which are both a result of a dysregulated immune system. You didn't give your body a chance to do its job.

Wanting to ease our pain or the pain of a loved one is a healthy, empathetic response. Honor that impulse. It is good and right. But instead of doping our bodies up with drugs when we get sick, we and our loved ones would be better off savoring the infection.

Pathogens often find a home in your respiratory tract or bowels, nice moist, friendly environments for our tiny, pathogenic companions. This is why being sick is the ultimate cleansing! Let your mucus flow. Cough. Sneeze. Go shit your brains out.

Think about it. Is it really a good idea to take a drug to stop diarrhea or vomiting when your immune system is just trying to push a pathogen out of your body? Instead, take a hot bath. Use herbs, which can help modulate the inflammation and make you more comfortable without suppressing the immune response. Do steams with a few drops of essential oils. Drink a lot of hot tea to keep your mucus moving. Yes to all of the above. An acute infection is your body's attempt to heal.

This is what we call working with the vitality in your body! When you get sick, your body is asking you to surrender to it and let it do its job.

Science is in its infancy of understanding what the immune system is capable of doing and how it works. Remember, you can respect something without understanding it. So next time you get sick, respect your immune system and get sick with all of your might.

Let your illness recreate you. Be reborn.

Come of out of the pain wiser and stronger.

For those of you who may be reading this and thinking, "But people used to die from high fevers and infections . . ."

Yes, you are right—they did, and still do. Often this is due to unsanitary conditions, or the case for those with underdeveloped or compromised immune systems and nutritional status, primarily in babies and elders. Yet, in developed countries we usually don't have those risks anymore. Help is there if you need it. All I'm saying is that the drug is a last resort. Give the body a fair chance at healing an acute infection on its own or you are setting yourself up for chronic disease.

Fever heals

I remember the first time I had a fever as an adult. I had almost completed my master's degree in herbal medicine, and was living in a basement apartment. I got a nasty virus that put me in bed for seven days and seven nights. I dealt with it by taking hot baths. Then I would wrap myself up in blankets and sweat. I drank herbal teas and took my supplements. Friends brought me food, which I barely ate. I was miserable and excited at the same time because I knew my body was cleaning house. After a childhood of suppressed infections, I got to watch my body work.

I was so disconnected from the outside world that when I finally went to the grocery store, an entire new season had emerged. In a week, Nature had shed the barren look of winter and replaced it with that bright, succulent green of spring, and I felt like I had, too. I felt so proud and empowered.

That pain of fever and of being sick, just like natural childbirth, catapults you into a higher version of yourself.

We have to find a way to restore the sanctity of acute

illness in our homes. Being sick is a sacred, transformative event. When you get sick, you are getting well. There are no shortcuts to healing. You must step out of the fear and into the wisdom of your body.

If you are a parent, you must do this first for yourself, and then steward your children's immune systems. Right alongside breastfeeding, well-managed acute childhood infections educate the child's immune system, gifting them with vitality for the rest of their lives.

Childhood illness

I talked with a colleague the other day about the importance of fevers and acute illness, specifically in children, and she told me a story about her son.

When he was 7 years old or so, he got so sick he started hallucinating. Both she and her husband are acupuncturists, so they were equipped to trust and handle the situation with the respect that we are discussing here. They stayed by his side, let him sleep, and made sure he was as comfortable as possible without compromising the process. They argued about going to the doctor (in the end, they didn't). And when the cycle of infection was complete, they said he actually looked different. More mature. His features had sharpened. He had actually grown physically.

Now, you may be thinking that this is what trauma does to a child, and that no 7-year-old child should "be more of a man." But that sort of trauma is unusual, and not in the normal order of things. Childhood infections, on the other hand, are a part of a healthy childhood. They are a natural part of the physical and spiritual maturation process.

That said, I also want to point out that growth spurts stress the body, leaving it more vulnerable to infections. So while this could be a chicken and egg phenomenon, it doesn't matter. Either way, the point is to trust the process and not interfere.

Being sick, like experiencing childbirth without the dulling effects of painkillers, is a rite of passage that we have lost in our modern world, to our detriment.

You cannot afford to be a victim and to be uninformed about how your body works. Vitality is your birthright. Experiencing acute illness is a part of that vitality. Take a stand for it—you're worth it.

Acute illness is not a sign of weakness; it is the body getting strong.

Now that you understand that every time you get sick, you're given a chance to heal, ask yourself: what am I going to do next time?

I get it. Learning to trust your body can be scary. Every time I get sick I wonder: "Will this ever end? Is this it . . . am I dying? Ugh. Get me out of here!" Dramatic, I know, and a direct result of the inflammatory cascade going on inside the body. Your body wants you to lay low. In technical language, this is called sickness behavior. Many people who are living with Lyme disease, chronic fatigue, or fibromyalgia are in this state. It is difficult beyond words because you may look healthy, and people just don't sympathize.

If you are going to embark upon the path of embracing your acute infection (and I hope you do), the first thing you must do is find a medical doctor who practices functional medicine, or a holistic health professional who understands that fever is the body's therapy. It is not the problem, and antibiotics and anti-inflammatory drugs should be a last resort. You need a healthcare professional by your side who you trust and is willing to help you. And if you are interested in learning more about how the physical body relates to mental function and spiritual development, check out the work of Rudolf Steiner, who founded the Waldorf Schools.

In an article titled "Childhood Vaccinations: An Anthroposophic Medical Perspective," author Peter Hinderberger says:

> "An infection that is allowed to follow its natural course may actually strengthen the child. Each time a pathogen enters the body through natural means (the so-called host invasion), there is an individualized pathophysiologic chain of events: incubation period, prodromal (forerunner symptoms), acute manifestation of disease, detoxification, elimination, and acquisition of immunity. In this process, all four members of the human organism, as described by Rudolf Steiner—the physical, etheric (energetic), and astral bodies, and the ego—are fully engaged. The result is strengthening of the whole organism."[12]

A word on childhood infection

The greatest risk during a fever is dehydration and blood sugar dysregulation, particularly in children whose bodies are small and vital. Things happen fast. In their *Nourishing Traditions Book of Baby and Childcare*, Sally Fallon and Dr. Tom Cowan do an excellent job of outlining the guidelines of healthy fever management. Every parent should read this book and have it on their bookshelf as a reference. It is extremely useful. At the same time, it is imperative that you partner with a health professional who understands and is trained in these matters.

Sometimes we need to build trust through another person.

The best thing you can do for your child's immune system is to breastfeed. I am very proud to say that Drake has never had a bottle, and I nursed him for four years. Breasts have glands that make antibodies against whatever microbes come along.

You cannot get this immune support in a formula, and while pumping is a noble pursuit, it falls short as well.

Katie Hinde, a biologist and associate professor at the Center for Evolution and Medicine at the School of Human Evolution & Social Change, Arizona State University, was asked, "How exactly is my body able to write my daughter a prescription for her illness without a diagnosis?" Hinde explained:

"When a baby suckles at its mother's breast, a vacuum is created. Within that vacuum, the infant's saliva is sucked back into the mother's nipple, where receptors in her mammary gland read its signals. This 'baby spit back-wash' . . . contains information about the baby's immune status. Everything scientists know about physiology indicates that baby spit backwash is one of the ways that breast milk adjusts its immunological composition. If the mammary gland receptors detect the presence of pathogens, they compel the mother's body to produce antibodies to fight it, and those antibodies travel through breast milk back into the baby's body, where they target the infection."[13]

However, even breastfeeding will not prevent your child from ever getting ill. In our home, when one of us gets sick, we stand back and let the immune system do its job. We do not have over-the-counter drugs in our house. We have a natural medicine cabinet filled with herbs and foods that empower the body.

Traditional wisdom says to feed a cold and starve a fever. We eat hot soups and drink hot tea when we are sick. Fasting is your friend when you have a fever. This is pretty easy because your appetite usually decreases when you have a fever. Your body has better things to do than eat when you are sick. Remember, your digestive tract and your immune system are inseparable!

In the early stages of a fever, when we feel cold and experience chills. That means the hypothalamus in our brain has dialed up the thermostat, but the body has not had time to respond. Drinking hot ginger-and-cinnamon tea with lemon and honey will help the body increase its temperature and ease those chills.

Sometimes we may skip chills and go directly into

a fever, where our skin becomes warm to the touch and rather dry. A cooling peppermint tea is perfect here, opening the pores of the skin and allowing the body to sweat, essentially "breaking" the fever.

Hydrotherapy is another wonderful way to work with chills and fevers. Hot baths combined with drinking hot tea can bring on the heat, while a cold bath, a cold compress on the forehead, or cold socks will work like a charm to lower it.

Your body is malleable. Use these tools to give it the ability to do its job.

As your immune system exercises its power, you will become more spiritually present, awake, and alive.

Allow yourself an excused absence

When I talk about the importance of convalescence, most people look at me funny, as if to say, "What are you talking about?" Nobody talks about this anymore because our world does not allow it.

All we hear is that getting sick is inconvenient. It's best not to get sick. And when you do, let's get you back to work as soon as possible.

It is a message seen on roadside billboards as we drive.

It's on the television.

It's in doctor's offices.

It's even present in the holistic health movement. "Just take more of these herbs and supplements and you won't get sick!" Well, that may be helpful sometimes, but not all the time.

Our bodies are sick because our minds are sick. We are so caught up in our lives that we forget the somewhat harsh reality that the world will go on without us.

When you die, the world will go on without you.

When you get sick, the world will go on without you.

I realize that people need to go to work to make money, and that days lost to illness are lost wages. As I've said before, the problems with our social structures are beyond the scope of this book. But when I look at the big picture of socioeconomics and its relationship to stress in this country, I despair. These problems run deep. But even in poverty, you can try to make different decisions. I just want you to be aware of this reality, so that next time you get sick, you can create the best level of convalescence that you possibly can.

What is convalescence, anyway? It is defined as "time spent recovering from an illness; recuperation."

"Time spent recovering" means not only going to bed when you are acutely ill, but also staying in bed after the fact. That's right . . . when you start to feel good, stay in bed. Give your body the space and time to fully recuperate. A major event just happened! Slow down and give your body the chance to integrate this healing.

Maybe you have to go to work or else you lose your job. I understand that it is hard in this country, especially during an economic downturn, to find a progressive company that puts an employee's needs before profit. But you also need to look at your life and ask questions. Am I a victim of my circumstances? Do I have choices that I haven't considered that would give me more freedom? Is there a different job I could pursue? A different company I could work for? Could I work from home? If change isn't possible, then maybe you go to work, skip all other activities, and get in bed and rest on your days off.

Do what you can with what you have.

I could not have violated this concept more when I had the mononucleosis infection that landed me in the hospital. Four days after my formal diagnosis, my boyfriend and I moved from Texas to California! I was so ill equipped to make this move that I had mild panic attacks while driving, and we had to stop the car so that my hands would stop shaking.

Everyone discouraged me from going, but I did not listen. I now see that my willfulness was the cause of my getting sick. I was not listening to my body. I was sick in my head. I had pushed myself to my absolute limits and my body would never be the same. It took me years to realize that if I would only stop pushing, my body could teach me how to live. Our culture's emphasis on determination and persistence comes at a very high cost.

We sell our souls.

Learning how to be sick well will help you reclaim your Spirit in a world gone completely mad.

Empower your immunity

Managing acute illnesses well prevents chronic inflammatory diseases. Currently there is an exponential increase in autoimmune disease, both in the number of people it affects and the types of these diseases, like rheumatoid arthritis, Hashimoto's, or scleroderma.

Often, those who suffer from these illnesses are told by their doctor, "You have an overactive immune system and your body is attacking itself."

No! No! No!

You have a confused, uneducated immune system. The body doesn't make mistakes.

What educates the immune system?

Not vaccinations.

Well-managed acute illnesses create a strong immune system.

Nobody knows the exact cause of autoimmune disease. It is complex, which is exactly why it eludes the medical system. Doctors tend to look for the one aberrant pathway in the body to find the one drug to fix it, but it's not that simple. There is some evidence of what we call molecular mimicry, whereby a pathogen looks like your tissue, which prompts the immune system to attack both.

What a bummer. But this is definitely not a mistake.

The corticosteroid and anti-inflammatory drugs that the medical system uses to treat autoimmune disease end up disabling the very thing that could save you: your immune system. Inflammation is your immune system at work. I have heard numerous testimonies of autoimmune diseases going into remission after an acute infection with a high fever.

I am very grateful for the medical system's anti-inflammatory tools. As I said before, if it weren't for inhalers and steroid shots, I would not be here right now. But if someone had had this conversation with my parents about food, food sensitivities, sleep, exercise, and convalescence, I would not have needed the inhalers in the first place.

The only thing you can change in this entire world is YOU.

Next time you get sick, give your body the chance to heal. You will be rewarded in unimaginable ways.

A final note regarding acute infections

When you come out of a well-managed flu or fever, pay attention to what kinds of foods you are craving. A few days of semi-fasting can begin to point to your food sensitivities. When you fast, you experience the food elimination diet described earlier. After I was sick, I used to crave toast and ice cream, sometimes both. Now I know that my body wanted to re-establish its normal inflammatory state. Don't let this wisdom slip by. Keep your observer intact at all times.

Your body is your best teacher.

Just like life.

CHAPTER 8

LIVE IN PEACE

*"We do not think ourselves into new ways of being;
we live ourselves into new ways of thinking."*

—RICHARD ROHR

Holding hands with fear

When my son was three, he was swinging on his swing set. As I pushed him, suddenly the swing broke. Just like that. Boom. My son had that "Help me, Momma!" look on face, but I really couldn't do anything. Time slowed down, and I watched him hit the wooden post and fall to the ground. My husband came running over. I immediately unstrapped my screaming son, took him out of the seat, and saw that he was ok physically but very scared. I held him and once he calmed down, gave him my breast. All was well. We felt very lucky.

In four seconds, our whole world could have changed. Drake could have fallen on his head. He could have broken his back. Freak accidents happen all the time. Life is uncertain. There is no safety in this world.

So where does this leave us?

Not where you might think. It sounds scary, but it is actually liberating.

Naming things, including truths, is healing. When you name something, you can work with it. At any given moment, we are weighing our options.

This is more important than that.

That is more important than this.

That doesn't make sense, given what I know.

This does make sense, given what I know.

What is everybody else doing? (Now, *that* one can get you into trouble sometimes.)

The problem is that many people are unconscious and often uneducated. They are living in fear, often watching too much television, running around making decisions from the lizard part of their brains. They are in survival mode. The prefrontal cortex, the thinking part of the brain, is out of the game. We have to pull that thinking mind back in, and I think the only way to do this is to name it: we are scared because we know there is no safety.

A former client of mine contacted me because she works in the medical system and was troubled by some of my anti-vaccination posts on Facebook. She said words to the effect of, "Look, I know you. I respect your work, but how could you do this? How could you put your child's life at risk like that? And then how could you promote it and recommend that other people take that path? Help me understand."

I explained that my goal is always to educate. When trying to make the very personal decision about whether or not to vaccinate their children, most people have not reviewed all the information on the issue. I simply make that information easily available. And once people are fully informed, they often make a different decision than the one they might have.

We also talked about the risks of home birthing, and the practice of giving newborns a vitamin K shot to prevent what's called Vitamin K Deficiency Bleeding (VKDB), which can be fatal. From her perspective, this was a no brainer—give it! My husband and I opted to administer vitamin K drops under my son's tongue. She thinks that was shortsighted.

I understand where my friend is coming from. In her work, she sees horrible things every day that trouble both of us. She sees how people who call themselves naturo-paths or holistic medicine practitioners take things too far. They may need medical treatment but choose not to get it. Parents wait so long to treat a baby's little injuries that they turn into gangrene.

I am so grateful we are able to communicate civilly about some pretty controversial matters. In the community of health practitioners, these are the topics that polarize us. But they are not black and white issues. As our conversation ensued, I kept thinking that we were both right; neither one of us was wrong. Since we were both well informed, what could be the difference underlying our respective decision-making process? What was fueling our perceptions? It hit me like a freight train:

People live in fear and seek solace in the illusion of safety.

She and I were simply choosing to follow different paradigms.

For example, having a baby is risky business. Anything could happen. Mom could die. Baby could die. There could be significant complications. Giving birth is risky no matter where you have the baby. I chose to take my chances at home, as women have done for millions of years, because I trust that women are designed to give birth and I do not feel safe in a hospital. Many women do feel safe in a hospital, and they would likely have a more positive birth experience there. But in either setting, things can go wrong.

If tragedy occurs during a home birth, proponents of

hospital births might say, "See. She should've had that baby in the hospital."

If tragedy occurs during a hospital birth, proponents of home births might say, "Oh, I could have told you that was going to happen. She should've had that baby at home with a midwife."

My question to you is: what the fuck do we know? Neither midwives nor hospitals can guarantee a 100% safe outcome. Sometimes shit goes down, and there is no way out. It is unfair, and it sucks. Until we name this, we are trapped in the illusion of safety.

The reality is that we are not safe. Ever. And our attempts to create the illusion of safety can backfire horribly. A hospital can take what might have been a healthy birth at home and then one intervention leads to another intervention leads to another intervention, and the soon-to-be-mommy is lying there hooked up to machines wondering what is happening. The most transformative event of her life is lost to technology and the need to control.

What do most people do when they get sick? They run to the doctor, effectively saying, "Save me from this pain of being sick." The doctor may prescribe an antibiotic, which is rarely necessary. If you are in generally good health, your doctor and the antibiotics should not be your first line of defense against an infection. Most infections are self-limiting. As we discussed earlier, if given enough time, rest, and herbal and nutritional tools, your body will find resolution on its own. Yet our first impulse is to run to the person in the white coat out of fear, the need to control, and the desire to be comfortable.

But we don't grow when we are comfortable.

I now realize that one of the reasons I was motivated to make the changes necessary to heal from thirty years of asthma is because I stopped covering up my symptoms with steroids and antihistamines. I was using my Albuterol inhaler hourly, and I wanted to stop. I was very uncomfortable, which led me to make changes in my life, like cleaning up my diet and getting rid of my dog.

Some people do require medications (I clearly used to be one of them). Not everyone is eligible for a home birth. But there are many, many healthy people in this world who give away their power to institutions out of unexamined fear.

You know what's really scary? Driving your car. Our bodies were never designed to get in a metal box with wheels and move 80 mph down the road. Yet most people never think twice about driving to work. Meanwhile, a woman's body is designed to have a baby, but people are constantly trying to tell us that we shouldn't trust it to do its job. Some in my family totally freaked out when we told them we were having a home birth. (I did it anyway).

It's such a contradiction, isn't it? The message behind my family's response to my home birth was: you can't trust your body.

Fear will always be with us. It keeps us alive. I respect my fear. It serves a purpose, but it does NOT need to run the show called My Life. I'm learning to acknowledge the fears I have and then do what I need to do, despite them.

My husband is 27 years older than me, and I just turned 40. When I was four months pregnant, a man I barely knew at a party posed an unexpected question. After first offering congratulations, he cocked his head and asked, "But, tell me, are you prepared to be a single mother?"

I was flabbergasted. I can't even remember how I responded. I have rolled that rude question over and over in my mind so, so, so many times.

Am I prepared to be a single mother? Nope.

Am I prepared to be a married mother? Nope.

We don't know what life has in store for us. We have to learn from our past, plan for the future, and live in the moment. Life is a dance, and dancing is much easier when you eat well, drink well, poop well, move well, and get sick well.

The only reason I wrote this book is because I want to be here with you more than I want to hide. But it does come with risk.

Writing is not a casual task for me. Every time I do it and share my thoughts, I feel a little scared. What will they think of me? Then I set that thought aside, and I do it anyway. It is so healing.

As I reflect on my past, the reality is that I couldn't heal because I wasn't physically well enough to do what I am doing right now. It was difficult for my nervous system and body to put myself at risk. I couldn't handle it.

Well, those days are over.

I birthed our baby at the foot of our bed, and I ate my raw placenta, like a warrior goddess. My post-partum depression was not a disease. It was a period of spiritual transformation. Just like everything changed as I lay in that hospital bed so many years ago, I was now transformed into a mother. A new me had to emerge, and it was fucking hard.

When I get sick, I don't run to the doctor, I care for myself. I know my body is amazing and in most cases, will resolve the situation. When we get fevers in our home, we are excited to see our bodies at work, not scared.

To me, the question I repeatedly ask is: how close to Nature am I? There is freedom in this. No one is right. No one is wrong.

And that's the freedom I want for you. I have given you multiple tools to claim your vitality, so that you can then align yourself with a higher purpose and put yourself at risk.

Let's be physically, spiritually and mentally strong, so that we can fight the good fight.

On the other side of fear is a life worth living.

Embrace everything

Living in peace is about knowing that you are a part of the divine design of life. Each step is always preparing you for the next. Nothing is disconnected. Nothing. Everything has a purpose. I had to lose my vitality and myself in order to reclaim it.

Eating sugar and refined carbohydrates taught me how to eat real food.

Competitive swimming and triathlons taught me discipline.

Waiting tables taught me how to speak and give pre-sentations.

Getting sick with mononucleosis saved my life. I would still be asthmatic if I had not ended up in the emergency room with that acute infection.

Two rounds of severe depression, first when I was heal-ing from mono and then again after giving birth, were the hibernation of my soul. I went into the darkness to find my light. Parts of me died in that time so I could re-emerge a more complete, whole human being. My depression was healthy, not pathological.

Having my heart broken by three men in a nine-year time span taught me how to love myself.

Any one of these events could be labeled as a hardship, but instead each event was an opening for me to learn how to live. Each step led me to the next, saying fuck, fuck, fuck along the way.

Obviously, there are no guarantees in life. Life isn't about fair. Life is about living. You can do all of the "right" things and get sick. It is impossible to know what the future holds. But right now, in this very moment, you can make a decision to move towards vitality instead of away from it by using the concepts in this book. The entire Universe is within you. When you do something good for yourself, you are taking care of the world.

We have dominion over nothing and no one. You are not only a part of nature; you are a force of nature, made up of all the water, fire, air, and earth that you see around you.

We need to work with our bodies and with nature, and

stop trying to control the things we don't like, including our negative emotions.

We do not have dominion over our bodies, just as we do not have dominion over the earth. The only way to heal is to work with our bodies, not against them.

So many people talk about changing the world. Well, that starts with changing yourself. For me, that started with accepting the darkness as much as I sought the light. I cried a lot, but tears are cleansing, just a like a good storm.

When someone says that they don't cry, I am concerned, just as I am when people brag about not getting sick. I cry a lot.

I've always been one of those people. I used to resist it. Strong people don't cry, right?

If there is live music playing at Whole Foods, yes, I will be the one crying in the produce section. And, oh, how I long to be a pretty crier...you know, the person who just has a single tear drop fall from their eyes. Nothing more. Nope, that's not me either. My face contorts. My chin quivers. Then the snot starts to flow. I can't talk. It's so intense. I used to apologize for my tears, until I heard a lecture at an herbal conference. The presenter said, "If you are a crier, don't ever apologize for your tears because you are crying for someone who can't." At that point, I stopped apologizing. I now see the wisdom in tears as a way to connect to something much bigger than our selves. Tears are movement. Let them flow.

I stopped fighting the water within me. Now it moves

and I move with it. I went through a box of tissues writing this book, reliving all the pain and seeing all the beauty.

As I've shared with you, I have touched anger, grief, anxiety, and depression in ways that left me immobile, as I had to let go of certain relationships, dreams, sugar, a dog, and more, in an effort to pull myself out of an inflammatory cascade that was killing me.

But I could not think myself out of my distress. Another self-help book or seminar was not going to help me—my dark thoughts were coming from an inflamed body. Physiology often dictates our emotional experience of life. The lack of understanding around this creates shame and guilt in people who are already sick.

Sometimes positive thinking just doesn't work.

Before I realized how I was making myself ill with processed foods, caffeinated beverages, alcohol, sugar, excessive exercise, and the impact of a chronic infection, I took my feelings out on my loved ones.

I still do this today when I am not present to what is happening.

Any inflammation in my body has the potential to come out as anger at the people I love.

"Dammit. If you would just stop that, I wouldn't feel so stressed!"

Which is just another way of saying that if something were different on the outside, then I would feel different in the inside. And it is just not true.

When I had my spiritual experience with my herbal formula, nothing in my life had changed but me. Something shifted so profoundly overnight in my body that I felt happy to be in a Laundromat.

A Laundromat, not in a nice part of town.

A Laundromat, where I quietly and joyfully folded clothes.

Your happiness is not about your external environment. It's about the internal world that you create every day with the decisions you make.

Now, when I come across someone who is rude and pissed off at the world, whether I am in the car driving or at the post office, I see myself and think, "I'm sorry that your breakfast cereal turned you into an asshole today. Or maybe you didn't sleep last night. It's not your fault. I know how you feel. May you find a better way."

CONCLUSION

"Do the best you can until you know better.
Then, when you know better, do better."
—MAYA ANGELOU

E very ending is a beginning.

I am so honored that you read this book, and I can only hope that you will begin to see food, herbs, nature, life, and yourself in a new way.

Vitality is your birthright, and it takes work.

The technical definition of healing is "the process of making or becoming sound or healthy again." It's not easy.

You are fragile and incredibly resilient at the same time. That resiliency contains your body's ability to heal. The wisdom within you that made you sick can also make you well.

Think of yourself as an onion. If you learn to live in peace, you will spend your lifetime peeling back the layers of everything that makes you, you. Sometimes that process will make your eyes water. Your years will be filled with joy, laughter, tears, and pain. Know that it is perfect and as it should be.

From that perspective, give yourself time. You cannot force miracles. All you can do is make space for them. Your job is to do the work.

Every single day.

For the rest of your life.

My husband has a saying: "Let love radiate without regard for results." I would add, "Let love radiate FOR YOURSELF without regard for results."

The only question to ask is: "How close to Nature am I?" Every cell in your being will love you for this.

Learn to observe yourself and make connections

between how you choose to live your life and how well you feel. Look for small changes you can make. Big shifts usually don't happen overnight. It is about the direction you are moving in, not how fast you get there.

I was so mad about something the other day that I broke a jar of peanut butter, and cut my hand. Would I define that act as peaceful? Was I proud of my destruction? Nope. But there it is. That's what happened. We are complex and need time to process our emotions. We move in and out of peace because that is the human condition.

It took me seven years to unravel the mystery of my asthma. There were countless times that I wanted to give up, but even on my bad days I felt my vitality improving. I knew I was on the right track.

Don't fall for the illusions put forth by the media and the medical system. There is no shortcut to vitality and its path is full of paradox. Living a vital life means that you take the bull by the horns and simultaneously, let it go.

And you can expect that the Universe will test you over and over and over again.

The Universe will put you in a room with cake and donuts. What will you do?

You will encounter your food allergens at restaurants and ask the server to please take your plate back to the kitchen to fix it. You will sit there uncomfortably while everyone around you eats. It will suck. It will be worth it.

The Universe will ask you over and over and over again, "Are you serious?"

"Do you want this?"
"Do you want to feel fully alive?"
My answer was, is, and always will be: FUCK YES!
I do hope that your answer will be the same.

HUNGRY
FOR MORE?

**Come join our community of people
committed to vitality!**
Watch for upcoming classes in the Austin area and the
virtual world. Never miss a beat (or a good eat). Sign up
for my weekly newsletter by visiting my website:

www.charlottekikel.com

For daily inspirations, connect with me on social media:
Instagram - @eatinpeacewc
Facebook - Eat in Peace with Charlotte
See you soon!

ACKNOWLEDGMENTS

Scott James – author coach
Stephanie Land – editing
Sheila Parr – cover design and layout
Mimi Bardagjy – copyeditor

Having a group of healers take a stand for your vitality is powerful.

The people listed below are the main reason you have this book in your hands.

Meet my self-care team:

Dr. Mark Bans
www.emotionalenergetichealing.com

Michelle Brown
www.wildflowerswellness.com

Dr. Aaron Chapa
www.justlivewell.com

Barbara Christman
www.barbchristman.com

Shri Estes–Quantum Healings
www.shriestes.com

Dr. Scott Jurica
www.drscottjurica.com

Dr. Tina Lightner-Morris
www.lightbalancecounseling.org

Amanda Love
www.thebarefootcook.com

Amy Person
www.persontherapy.com

Dr. Ellie Phillips
www.drellie.com

Vanessa Rutkowski
www.tigerlilyacupuncture.com

Zero Gravity Institute
www.zerogravityinstitute.com

Many thanks to each of you!

YOUR EAT-IN-PEACE PLATE

What follows is not an exhaustive list of recommended foods, but a guideline for healthy choices. I realize that when it comes to remaking their diet, people need structure, particularly at first. With the exception of starchy vegetables and sweeteners, you can pretty much eat as much of these foods as you would like, so there is plenty of freedom within the boundaries.

You will see that I have listed vegetables in the order of their starch content. While I am not a fan of eating by numbers, I am a fan of awareness, and we generally underestimate how many carbohydrates we eat. The hormone used to regulate blood sugar is insulin, and it can be extremely inflammatory when circulating in excess. Eating in a way that does not provoke insulin benefits everyone's health.

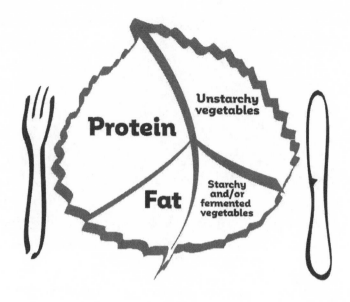

Carbohydrates are the only macronutrient (as compared to protein and fat) that our bodies do NOT need, but unfortunately they often make up the bulk of our diets. At a certain point, a person's metabolism can lose the ability to tolerate carbohydrates, even if the food is healthy. It's a good idea to do the math to have a general idea of how many carbohydrates you are consuming. 50–60 grams per day is desirable.

Eating twice as many vegetables as fruits, and having a serving of protein the size of your palm, are excellent rules of thumb, too.

Speaking of rules, please realize that all dietary interventions are really just personal experiments, asking the question: how does life show up for me when I make this change? Something can be great in theory, but not actually work. Something can be great for your neighbor, but not for you. That's ok. You're in charge.

I have also found that positive, sustainable dietary change takes time. There can be sharp right and left turns, no doubt, but in most cases there is a build-up of physical, emotional, and spiritual energy that occurs to give you the strength to make the change.

As I completed this book, I began a ketogenic diet, which is a high fat, adequate protein, low-carbohydrate way of life that will teach my body to use fat for energy. I've known for a long time that it would be my next step. It's taken me over two years to make the leap! But when I did, it was pretty darn effortless. Just like a seed planted in the ground turns into a plant, dietary transformation takes time. Be gentle with yourself and at the same time, expect great things through your effort.

From my experience, it all boils down to choosing based on foods you enjoy and foods that promote healthy blood sugar regulation and a healthy inflammatory response.

Fats
Butter/Ghee
Coconut oil
Lard/Tallow
Olive oil
Avocado oil

Protein

Fowl with skin on (chicken, duck, turkey, etc.)

Red meat (beef, bison, lamb, venison, etc.)

Cold-water fish and seafood (sardines, tuna, wild salmon, etc.)

Pork

Vegetables (listed from lowest to highest carbohydrate content)

3% or fewer carbohydrates

Asparagus

Bamboo shoots

Bean sprouts

Beet greens

Bok choy greens

Broccoli

Cabbages

Cauliflower

Celery

Chicory

Collard greens

Cucumber

Endive

Escarole

Garlic

Kale

Kohlrabi

Lettuces

Mushrooms
Mustard greens
Parsley
Radishes
Salad greens
Spinach
String beans
Summer squashes
Turnip greens
Watercress
Yellow squash
Zucchini squash

6% or fewer carbohydrates
Bell peppers
Bok choy stems
Chives
Eggplant
Green beans
Green onions
Okra
Olives
Pickles
Pimento
Rhubarb
Sweet potatoes
Tomatoes
Water chestnuts
Yams

7–9% or fewer carbohydrates
Acorn squash
Artichokes
Avocado
Beets
Brussels sprouts
Butternut squash
Carrots
Jicama
Leeks
Onion
Pumpkin
Rutabagas
Turnips
Winter squashes

12–21% or fewer carbohydrates
(consume only 2–3 times per week)
Chickpeas
Horseradish
Jerusalem artichokes
Kidney beans
Lima beans
Lentils
Parsnips
Peas
Potatoes

Fermented vegetables
Sauerkraut
Kimchee
Miso
Tempeh

Fruits/Nuts/Snacks
Seasonal, local fruits
Berries
All nuts and seeds, except for peanuts
Dark chocolate with 71% or higher cocoa content

Beverages
Filtered water
Green tea
Herbal teas
Apple cider vinegar diluted with water
Kombucha
Homemade broth (vegetable, chicken, or bone)
Coconut water or kefir

Healthy Sweeteners (use sparingly)
Maple syrup
Honey
Coconut sugar
Stevia
Xylitol (from birch trees)

I mentioned earlier that in an ideal world, we would grow, hunt, or raise the food that we eat. Not many people in our modern world live this way. So the next best thing is buying food directly from farms, or shopping at farmer's markets. There are many online vendors available for good food. The Weston A. Price Foundation publishes a shopping guide annually that will help you discover a world of healthy food options. I buy some of our foods online and have them shipped directly to our home. That said, I always prefer to support local businesses.

When it comes to produce, sometimes I get the question: local or organic? I say local, and here's why. You want to eat plants that have adapted to your environment for three reasons. First, no matter where you are, local foods are fresher. Secondly, as I explained in chapter 3, plants can't move, so they have to make protective chemicals in order to survive. These are called secondary plant metabolites and often taste bad. I talked about tannins, for example, which are bitter and astringent. If you recall, when a cow comes along, alfalfa will make more tannins to make the cow leave it alone. In our bodies, tannins can offer immune support by binding to pathogenic bacteria in the gut. They can also support the function and healing of mucus membranes, particularly during infections and healing from leaky gut. We directly benefit from these plant adaptations. Third, eating local can support your microbiome. One of the many things that connect us to our environment is the bacteria in and on our bodies and all around us. In that sense, eating locally means that you are supporting your immune system and digestive function.

If you really want to take it to the next level, seek out biodynamic foods, which are foods grown in a holistic and ecologically sound method pioneered by Rudolph Steiner, a philosopher and founder of the Waldorf School. I often describe biodynamic foods as beyond organic, and as it turns, I am not far from the truth.

My friend Bill McCranie owns Chickamaw Farms in Bastrop, Texas, where my family goes every year to pick his amazing blueberries and purchase his beef. He explains:

> "Biodynamic farming is what organic farming was 40 years ago. It's a way of living and helping the planet, not just growing food. Preparations are used and rituals are performed to bring about a more holistic concept and application to the farm and ranch. These preparations are made from fermented cow manure, minerals, flowers and herbs to restore, invigorate and harmonize the life forces on the land. Biodynamic practices also include the use of influences from the greater cosmos in order to bring it all into line with soil, plant, and animal health. This enhances the nutrition, quality, and flavor of the food being raised."

I can certainly attest to that. Bill's blueberries glow and his beef is delicious.

FREQUENTLY ASKED QUESTIONS

Here are the 11 of the most frequently asked questions I have encountered over the years.

1. Canned or frozen?

Fresh and local is always your best bet, and next on the list is frozen. Frozen vegetables endure minimal processing and are often very appealing for single or elderly people who need small servings. They are also frozen at their peak ripeness, making some even tastier than fresh, which can lose some nutritive value in transit or in the store. That said, I do use canned foods sometimes. Just be aware that canned foods are often higher in sodium and have preservatives, and the can's plastic lining may contain bisphenol A (BPA), which can cause hormonal imbalances if consumed regularly.

2. If I eliminate dairy, how will I get my calcium?

Sesame seeds. Leafy greens. Figs. Nuts.

Calcium is a ubiquitous mineral. You will be fine and so will your bones.

Speaking of healthy bones, weight-bearing exercise is just as important to your vitality as nutrition. Bone is a living tissue that must remain strong and slightly supple at the same time.

3. Carbohydrates are getting a really bad rap. Why can't I eat bread? Isn't it the staff of life?

Or the staff of death . . . depending on who you are. In my case, I damaged my carbohydrate metabolism by eating too much sugar. Some genetic lines, like Native Americans, Hawaiians, and Eskimos, do not tolerate carbohydrates well at all, and develop diabetes as a result of eating our modern, carbohydrate-heavy diet. In addition, some people develop sensitivity to gluten, the proteins found in many grains that gives bread its elasticity and chewiness. Some people's lives are totally changed by removing gluten-containing foods.

And then there's the fact that carbohydrates, under various guises like corn syrup, evaporated cane juice, and anything ending in -ose, show up in all sorts of foods where they don't belong, like ketchup, nut butters, pasta sauces, yogurts, and salad dressings. We can blame the low-fat movement of the 1980s that dictated that fat is bad. But fat makes food taste good, and it satisfies the appetite. When you take the fat out of a food product, you then have to add sugar to make it taste good. Sugar is obviously a carbohydrate. Food manufactures started marketing "low-fat" products that only tasted good because of the amount of sugar loaded into them. Americans, big on snacks and not yet big on home cooking, were led to believe they could eat all the processed food they wanted and still be eating healthy. As we grew fatter and fatter, it was clear this wasn't so. "You can't eat just one" is a real phenomenon!

Here's how I would rank carbohydrates, from best to worst:

Unstarchy vegetables

Starchy vegetables

Fruit (berries are a particularly good choice)

Legumes

Grains (corn is a grain, not a vegetable)

If you are going to eat bread, sourdough is best, and if you can learn to bake it yourself, even better. You can refer to the Weston A. Price Foundation for how to properly prepare grains. Or you may end up prescribing to the paleo way of life, which claims that since early humans didn't eat beans and grains, our bodies weren't designed to digest them, and therefore we probably shouldn't eat them, either.

It all depends on who you are! You have to find your own personal truth under the umbrella of the universal truth: eat real food.

If you thrive on looking at numbers, then aim to consume approximately 50–60 grams of carbohydrates per day, not counting unstarchy vegetables. Although I do not advocate counting calories, this is an excellent exercise for getting a sense of what you actually consume. Many underestimate the amount of carbohydrates they eat, and excessive consumption is a symptom of carbohydrate dependency or addiction.

Just keep in mind that you are not a machine. Diets are not a mathematical solution to whatever ails you. We tend to think that 1 + 2 = 3 in terms of weight loss and health: If I eat one way, then this will be the result. I will tell you right now that the body doesn't work like that.

Sometimes you get sick before you get better.

Sometimes you gain weight or maintain your weight when you want to lose it.

Don't ever forget that your body is smarter than you. It doesn't care what you look like, and weight isn't an adequate measure of health, anyway.

4. But won't fat make me fat?

Nope. The calories in/calories out theory is dead. Gone. Goodbye. Insulin is what makes you fat. Insulin is a hormone secreted by the pancreas in the presence of sugar in the blood. Insulin gets the sugar into the cell for fuel. Or not. If you eat too many carbohydrates, insulin receptors down regulate and your cells starve, while you gain weight. Where there is insulin, there is insulation—you cannot burn fat when insulin is present. Fat does not demand insulin to metabolize, and it promotes a feeling of calm in your nervous system. Sugar excites the brain; fat calms it down. This is why the medical system recognizes the ketogenic diet—which teaches your body and brain how to run on fat for fuel—as a viable therapy for seizures. Fat will not make you fat; it will make you happy!

But let's be honest. We need to move past the "will this food make me fat?" conversation completely. You eat food because it feeds your vitality, not because you are trying to control the number on a scale.

5. What about cholesterol?

What about it?

Cholesterol is your friend. It is the precursor to every hormone in your body, including your sex and stress hormones. It creates structure in your cellular membranes. It performs immune and anti-inflammatory functions. It protects you. It has never been and will never be the cause of disease. When you eat cholesterol, your body makes less, so the notion that you can lower your cholesterol through diet is inherently flawed.

Ultimately, cholesterol is a story of shooting the messenger. High cholesterol may be correlated with chronic disease, but that does not mean it is the cause. It is easy to measure on blood work and then it's easy to lower with statin drugs. So you watch your numbers change, and the doctor says, "You're doing great!" The problem is that cholesterol is not the enemy, but then you lack the motivation to change your diet and lifestyle.

By the way, it is a healthy habit to be very suspicious whenever a doctor wants to medicate a number, including blood pressure. It's an easy sale to people who are ignorant of how their body functions.

If you would like to learn more about this specific topic, there are a number of excellent books about cholesterol in the appendix titled My Library.

6. Isn't plant-based protein superior to animal-based protein?

No. We evolved eating meat, particularly fatty meat. This is not debatable. It is a fact. And the longer we debate it, the sicker people are getting. You are here today because someone before you ate some form of animal protein. I eat a healthy serving of animal protein three times per day. Sometimes that shift alone will help you feel like a million bucks.

And it's not all about essential amino acids. It's also

about the fat. Essential fatty acids are essential because your body can't make them and the most absorbable form is found in fish and food made from pastured animal. Vitamin A is only found in animal foods. Plant foods, like carrots and sweet potatoes, contain beta-carotene, which is a precursor to vitamin A, and the conversion of beta-carotene to vitamin A is not certain. Babies lack the enzyme to make the conversion and excessive insulin levels will block it as well. This is why you put butter or ghee on your orange vegetables! The fat aids the absorption of the beta-carotene.

The Weston A Price Foundation and the Price-Pottenger Nutrition Foundation do an incredible job of educating people on this subject matter.

Most people have heard the wisdom of shopping on the perimeter of the grocery store for the perishable items, and that you should eat a rainbow of colors from the vegetable kingdom. All that is good and well, but as I've stated previously, here is another thought for you: eat a rainbow of meats and fish! Pastured beef, buffalo, pork, lamb, duck, venison, liver, wild salmon, rabbit, and chicken are all viable options.

People need a variety of healthy meats and fish as much as they need a variety of plants. They have different amino acid and nutrient profiles, and different ways of providing energy. Lamb is very warming for people with a colder constitution, beef builds the blood, and easy-to-digest white fish is a wonderful choice for convalescence.

If you are a vegan or a vegetarian, and you have read this far, thank you. As I've said before, I salute you for caring about what you put into your body and for your concern for the environment. But please know that your plant-based diet is likely to fail you at some point, and it most certainly fails our children. That way of eating can only serve you for so long as an adult, and it doesn't serve fertility or the healthy development of babies and children at all. In fact, it can cause irreversible damage.

7. I've heard that I need to eat every two hours. Is that true?

Snacking is a temporary solution to your problem. Snacking is compensatory to poor blood sugar regulation. Do you remember when mothers used to tell their children: "No snacking! You're going to ruin your dinner!" There is truth to this. We need to have empty stomachs. When insulin declines, growth hormone comes out to play, which burns fat and maintains lean muscle mass. If you eat all day long, that never happens! If you are attempting to repair your endocrine system from years of abuse due to sugar and carbohydrate consumption, then snacking may serve you during the repair process, but it is not a long-term solution.

I remember when I felt hunger in my stomach for the very first time. It was a few days after I had my spiritual experience with the herbal formula. I was studying at my desk and had totally lost track of time. Looking up at the clock, I saw that it was three o'clock, and though I hadn't eaten since breakfast and my stomach was growling, I felt fine. For 30 years, I had felt hunger in my nervous system. As my blood sugar would vacillate, I would experience hunger as a general irritability. But not that day. I was so liberated! Yes, this is normal hunger! I'm not angry, I'm just hungry!

The best way to stop snacking and reclaim physiological and emotional stability is to eliminate carbohydrates before noon. Start with a breakfast composed of good quality protein and fat.

To give you a reference point, aim for 35 grams of protein for breakfast, drenched in fat. There are 7–8 grams of protein in an egg, which is the equivalent of an ounce of meat.

Think sausage and eggs.

Bacon and eggs.

Steak and eggs.

Frittata.

Breakfast tacos using paleo-style tortillas.

Chicken with the skin on, and a few slices of avocado.

A salmon patty with a fried egg on top.

Leftovers from dinner.

Let me explain the importance of this to you. If you eat dinner at 6 p.m. and can save your carbohydrates for lunch and dinner, you then have the opportunity to forgo an insulin response for 18 hours out of a 24-hour day, and you won't need to snack. Excessive insulin is at the root cause of most of our modern illnesses and exacerbates any inflammatory condition.

This breakfast changes lives.

Of course, pregnancy and breastfeeding throw all these anti-snacking guidelines out the window. In that season of fertility and reproduction, snacking can be your friend.

See that, right there? This is what makes everyone crazy. Context is EVERYTHING!

8. How can I make sense of my cravings for certain foods?

First, let's remember the phenomenon around food sensitivities: your body wants to maintain balance. When a specific food creates inflammation, the body now has a new set point and will crave the food that is causing a problem. This is no different than an alcoholic or drug user craving their next hit. The only answer is to withdraw the likely foods from your diet and observe your body.

Second, consider the possibility that cravings come from a dietary fat deficiency. I first heard this in a lecture by Dr. Tom Cowan, author of *The Fourfold Path to Healing*. I resisted this idea until I started to pay closer attention to the context of my cravings. Sure enough, not eating enough good-quality fats (in the form of olive oil, coconut oil, butter or ghee, lard, nuts and seeds) makes me crave strange foods, like pepperoni pizza! Consuming animal protein can play a role here, too, but fat is just as, if not more, important. Fat satiates the appetite and makes you feel good!

You need to understand that eating fat promotes oxytocin. Oxytocin is the hormone of calm, love, and connection and is dominant during labor (where it facilitates contractions) and breastfeeding (where it facilitates bonding). It also opposes the stress response.

When we eat food high in fat, the upper part of the small intestine releases a hormone called cholecystokinin (CCK). CCK not only activates gall bladder function, it also stimulates the release of oxytocin, giving us a feeling of satiety and well-being after eating fat.[14]

Third, sugar and caffeine are drugs. If you ingest a drug, expect to crave it. If you crave true freedom, however, remove these substances entirely. With time, your body will adjust to life without them, and you will feel amazing.

No one can reach his or her dietary goals on willpower alone. As a source of energy, willpower is limited. Some people have very little of this energy and others appear to have more, but going it on willpower alone will eventually fail you.

The real way to address food cravings is to call upon something much, much larger than your self. This is at the heart of the 12-Step programs.

When recovering, your vitality becomes more important than eating dessert. That is a different kind of fuel than willpower. Committing fully to your vitality makes it much easier to refuse certain foods because then, you realize that your choices are changing the world. You access an energy that is of Spirit, not of the ego. This is the flow that will sustain you.

Fourth, as previously mentioned, eat a breakfast rich in fat and protein. Throw away your cereal, toasts, smoothies, oatmeal, donuts, and bagels, and enter the realm of eggs, sausage, bacon, leafy greens, quiche, breakfast tacos, and butter coffee. If I stray from my egg and sausage breakfast, I am amazed at how hungry I am at dinner, and then the cravings for weird food hits me in the early evening.

The only way to know this is to do it.

Fifth, if the food you are craving exists in Nature, go for it! There is probably something that your body needs in that food. Honor it.

However, if a processed food keeps haunting you, take a deeper look at adding more fat and protein to your diet, pumping up your breakfast, and investigating your relationship to inflammatory foods, like wheat, dairy, corn, and soy.

Sixth, cultivate compassion for yourself. If you "give in" to your cravings, avoid the spiral of shame. We are complex human beings, and must repeatedly forgive ourselves and start over.. These forces working within us are strong (consider hormonal fluctuations with the menstrual cycle), and it's not the end of the world if you eat the cookie or brownie or whatever else you're yearning for. Just make sure that it is the best cookie you can get your hands on!

9. How do I read a food label?

Ideally, we would not consume foods that have labels. The first challenge is to stop paying attention to the breakdown of carbohydrates, protein, and fats. Companies engineer food products to have a desirable macronutrient profile, but it doesn't make their product food. Look at the list of ingredients, and then ask questions like: Can I find this in nature? Could I theoretically make this at home? Were these ingredients once alive? If the answer is no, then it is not likely to be food.

10. Can you tell me more about choosing healthy sweeteners?

Here's the list of sweeteners listed from worst to best, and my rationale for ranking them:

Artificial sweeteners: These are man-made chemicals that burden detoxification pathways, along with our nervous and immune systems. In addition, studies have shown that these sweeteners dsyregulate appetite and result in weight gain,[15] making you eat more later. Think about it: you put a sweet taste on your tongue and your body expects nutrition to follow. But in this case there is none. Why wouldn't that make you hungrier?

High fructose corn syrup (HFCS): Another sweetening agent made in the laboratory with a genetically modified grain. It's cheap, and processed "food" and drink manufacturers love that. It significantly damages our livers and mechanisms that regulate our blood sugar. Fatty liver disease used to be a diagnosis for alcoholics. Not any more, thanks to HFCS. It is a Franken-food that should be avoided at all costs.

Refined sugar: Although this sweetener is naturally occurring, unlike the two above, its manufacturing process strips sugar of everything nature intended and creates a delicious white crystal. This crystal is a drug: "intense sweetness can surpass the cocaine reward."[16] When scientists give mice a choice between sugar water and cocaine, guess which they choose? Sugar water. Brain scans have shown that sugar lights up the reward centers in the brain more than cocaine. Refined sugar and refined flour are the recipe for heart disease, diabetes, and obesity, and an overall unfulfilling life. The problem is that in our modern world sugar has become a health food, so you have to read labels. Health food stores are full of "natural foods" that contain unnatural sugar. Seriously, it is insane, and the marketing is brilliant.

If you want an in-depth look at this, read *The Case Against Sugar*, by Gary Taubes. He makes the argument that sugar is a toxin that creates disease over time.

Agave nectar, brown rice syrup, tapioca syrup: I admit that I am lumping these into one category, but they are all just more forms of sugar disguised as health foods—which pisses me off even more than usual, because people think they are choosing more wisely, when they are not. Found in lots of vegan, raw, and paleo-inspired foods, these should also be avoided because when they hit your blood stream, the body doesn't know that it came from our beloved brown rice, etc.—it just sees sugar. And it's hard for me to talk about agave "nectar," which implies that it just came out of the plant. No, it didn't. It is a man-made syrup that is very high in fructose. The body has a hard time metabolizing high amounts of fructose.

Coconut sugar: This is the darling of the paleo community. Dark brown in color, it has some nutrients and may be friendlier on the glycemic index, but it's still sugar. Best delivered in very dark chocolate, don't you think?

Molasses: The good news is that this is definitely the most nutrient dense sweetener. The bad news is that it tastes like it! I'm sorry—I just haven't found a practical way of using molasses, and have ruined many recipes trying to make it work. If you can use it on a regular basis, I salute you. This is a good one.

Maple syrup: So now we are getting into the realm of healthy sweeteners that have a history, which means that they've been around a bit longer than some of our newer inventions, and are safe. This obviously comes from the sap of trees, but we can't glorify it too much because it is high in simple sugars. It has to be concentrated by boiling down to syrup, so some processing is necessary. That said, it is processing that can be done with human hands and heat.

Honey: Touted as a miracle food for its external and internal healing properties, honey is amazing and could almost be classified as a medicine. Its antibacterial properties are astounding. That said, use sparingly.

Xylitol: Make sure that what you buy comes from birch trees. I like this sweetener because it is lower in carbohydrates and is good for your teeth. Xylitol helps balance the bacteria in your mouth, getting rid of the bad guys and promoting the good ones. For the most part, you can use it just like you would sugar, as it is also a white crystal. I buy Xyla on Amazon. I also enjoy Zellies for a sweet way to clean my mouth during the day! Note: this is a sugar alcohol, so for some it may cause digestive upset or gas. Just pay attention to your body.

Stevia: This is a sweet gift from the herbal kingdom. I point out that it is an herb because some people can't stand the bitter after-taste of this plant. For that reason, I find that it works very well with sour things like lemon and cranberry. The bitterness just disappears into the sourness and all is well. I prefer the liquid extract, but powder can work well, too, and so can the dried leaves, particularly when steeping teas. Omica Organics is a good brand (the butterscotch flavor is delicious). With zero carbohydrates, this is one of the more appealing ways to sweeten your life.

There is another sweetener available now called luo han guo. It is powder made from monkfruit. I've heard it is as wonderful as stevia, but have not yet tried it.

I also want to say that no matter how healthy the sweetener is, it's still sweet, which means that many, many people will have a tendency to over-consume it.

In the presence of sugar addiction, everything sweet is a gateway drug.

We are so wired for the sweet taste. More than any other taste, this is THE one. Look at how rare it is in nature, and how it often appears with fiber. Berries, fruits, nuts and seeds, and even meat are considered sweet. Many of these are seasonal treats! I mean, do you really think all of our ancestors had access to maple trees or beehives or a sweet little stevia plant growing near by? Hell no!

The sweet taste is a slippery slope—it doesn't matter where it comes from.

Some people can be satisfied with one glass of wine, while others become alcoholics. Some people can have a little honey or maple syrup and it's no big deal, while others are going to have a problem. You have to know who you are, and I think we are all susceptible to the intoxicating taste of sweetness.

However, I will say this as well. When you eat a sweet treat, take my advice: sit down and enjoy it with no distractions. Savor it. Moan over it. Because pure pleasure is the purpose of these foods, so don't deny yourself.

11. Do I need to take supplements?

Yes! But you need to take the right kind of supplements. We need to eat food and supplement with food. There are two companies I rely on to deliver the best nutrition and herbal support for our bodies: Standard Process and Medi-Herb. Let me explain.

I want you to think about the fact that where you live is different from where you are from. We live and work in square buildings. These are protected environments designed to make us feel more comfortable. This is a noble pursuit, but comes with a cost.

These sterile environments separate us from where we evolved, which is outside in nature, where nothing is square. The shape of nature is one of spirals. There is flow and movement.

Not so with our houses and offices. These places are static. They are designed to stay the same.

Synthetic vitamins are a modern, chemical invention. They are the equivalent of our square buildings and controlled environments. They will not nourish our bodies or our souls. Only food can do that.

Synthetic vitamins, along with isolated constituents from herbs, are like processed foods. The body doesn't recognize them as whole and complete.

But you are whole and complete.

And you deserve whole and complete foods *and* supplements.

You are not a robot. You are a living, breathing, forever-evolving, adapting human being.

Consider the case of vitamin C, which we call ascorbic acid. Typically, you will pick up a vitamin C supplement in the store and see 500+ milligrams of vitamin C, but is this what nature intended? Does nature round off the amount of vitamins present in foods to the nearest zero? Nope—I don't think so! There is only about 40 mg of vitamin C in a grapefruit.

Vitamins occur in a complex in foods. The ascorbic acid is a small part of the vitamin C complex. It is the only part that supplement manufacturers can replicate in their laboratories. In nature's foods, ascorbic acid actually serves to protect what used to be called vitamin P, which stands for permeability. This vitamin P is now known as bioflavonoids. People with low vitamin C and bioflavonoid intake have less vascular integrity. Their capillaries bleed, turning their toothbrushes pink, and they bruise easily. These bioflavonoids that make up vitamin P are found in the bitter white part of citrus fruits. This is where your medicine is and you can taste it!

An isolated vitamin C supplement using high doses of ascorbic acid will fail your body. It lacks complexity and vitality. I could even take this one step further and say that synthetic vitamins are worse than processed foods; they are like pharmaceutical drugs. Drugs come in and push one pathway in the body, almost always depressing it, effectively saying, "Hey body, don't do that!"

So it goes with high doses of synthetic supplements. They may not always shut down a pathway, like a drug, but they will flood the pathway, depleting the body of the nutritional co-factors necessary for the body to utilize the vitamin. Foods from nature will never do this because foods in nature are complex, with lots of nutrients and co-factors in small amounts.

Stedman's Medical Dictionary defines vitamins as "one group of organic substances, present in minute amounts in natural foodstuffs, that are essential to normal metabolism" (p. 1567, 2005).

If you take a flower apart, you can't put it back together again. It loses its essence. The same can be said for real foods and herbs. We will never fully understand them by breaking them down into parts. We can't make flowers and we can't make real food. That is the realm of Nature and Spirit.

Human beings are dynamic forces of nature. You and I have so many different facets to our personalities and bodies—different temperaments, strengths, and weaknesses—and so it goes with food and herbs. Instead of respecting this complexity, we isolate what we think is the active part of the food or herb, and when we do so, we lose.

Instead of eating a steak, we buy a protein powder.

Instead of eating an orange, we take a vitamin C supplement with high doses of ascorbic acid.

Instead of using turmeric root, we take high doses of curcumin, which is just one part of a complex spice and herbal medicine.

What I am trying to say here is that you are a flower—Nature's unique expression of the human form. You deserve the complexity of what Nature has to offer in terms of nourishment. Don't fall for the hype of nutriceuticals. They promise everything and deliver nothing.

In 2006, I discovered whole food supplements from Standard Process and herbal medicine from MediHerb.

Both companies respect the complexity of nature and our bodies, facilitating healing on all levels: physical, emotional, and spiritual.

Remember what we previously discussed: the whole-food matrix hooks you into the univeral matrix.

In my case, after changing my diet and trying all the top-of-the-line professional brands of supplements, Standard Process and MediHerb products together put the finishing touch on my health. They helped me find the flow of life.

From an intellectual perspective, it is difficult to describe how these supplements work. You have to experience them. I discovered these supplements in herb school when one of my teachers said, "I don't have any financial ties to MediHerb. Kerry Bone [who is the founder] makes the best herbal medicine in the world." The next day I called Standard Process and set up an account.

I immediately grasped the power of the herbal products. Here is a company dedicated to finding the highest quality plant material and making the best medicine possible without the use of heat and chemicals. I have visited their facility in Australia. It is impeccable. When you taste their liquid herbs, you know the medicine is there, and when you open a bottle of their tablets, you can smell and see the plant.

Standard Process, however, was a mystery to me. The names of the products were weird—like Catalyn, Allerplex, and Cataplex G—and when I looked at the labels, I thought, "There's nothing in that! What is this stuff?"

I ended up following a protocol from Dr. Tom Cowan's book, *The Fourfold Path to Healing*. It offered immune and hormonal support using these products, and my health finally started to improve.

Every single month for about a year I had been getting sick before my menstrual cycle. Not sick from my period, but my immune system couldn't deal with the hormonal shifts, so I just became more susceptible to pathogens. I would get colds, the flu, and gastrointestinal bugs. I would miss work. It became a predictable mess. I was depressed from the repeated inflammatory cascades. After taking these supplements, two months went by and I didn't get sick, because I was now nutritionally fortified. Despite my lack of intellectual understanding, I discovered that these were very effective tools and they now had my attention.

I've continued to study the work of Dr. Royal Lee, who founded Standard Process in 1929. This is the oldest nutrition company in the United States. I mentioned earlier that MediHerb comes to us from Australia. When MediHerb decided to open the US market, they aligned with Standard Process as their distributor. This is a perfect match. Both of these companies successfully put Nature into bottles. Magnificent.

Eat food. Supplement with food. Nothing else makes sense.

Approximately 70% of the concentrated foods in Standard Process supplements are grown on their organic farm right at their headquarters in Wisconsin. This farm sits in the Kettle Moraine Valley, where glaciers deposited minerals into the soil millions of years ago.

Being from Texas, the first time I saw this soil I didn't know what it was—so dark and rich in color. I thought, "That's dirt?!" It didn't look real. Standard Process is a steward to the land. This is important to me. Synthetic vitamins are petroleum by-products from the coal tar industry, and if a company is using food in their products, most of them can't tell you where those ingredients even come from. Standard Process grows the vegetables in this amazing soil, harvests them at the peak of their nutritional value, and then processes them without the use of heat. When you visit their farm and manufacturing facility, their integrity is palpable.

Don't like beets or want to prepare them? Take Betafood.

Don't eat cruciferous vegetables, like kale, broccoli, and Brussels sprouts? Take Cruciferous Complete.

Those are the more simple products, but you see the beauty, yes? They are concentrations of foods that may be missing from your diet.

They also incorporate organs and glands into their products. Many people express concern about this. I celebrate it! Our ancestors ate the entire animal. All of it. Everything. Nothing was wasted. Not only that, but Native people and doctors of traditional medicine have recognized that "like heals like."

Got a heart problem? Eat heart.

Got a lung problem? Eat lung.

Got a liver problem? Eat liver.

This freaks out many people in our modern world. I must admit that I don't cook with organs and glands as much as I would like to. Fortunately, they are in these nutritional supplements. This is another reason they are so effective. No need to fear organs and glands—embrace them! Our ancestors certainly did.

If you value purity above the vitality that only nature can provide, then go ahead and use synthetic vitamins, isolated constituents from herbs and pharmaceutical drugs. That will be the only thing that makes sense, given your belief system. But I do think that you are missing something profoundly healing that can only be found in whole food nutrition. After all, what we find in synthetic vitamins is what we can identify and replicate. I want the unknown factors and those that we cannot replicate coming into my body as well.

Unfortunately there are many companies claiming to make whole food supplements. Buyer, beware! Many of these companies put high doses of synthetic vitamins in a base of yeast and call that whole food nutrition. It is not. What you will see on the label is 100% of the RDA, 150% of the RDA, 2,000% of the RDA, etc. You need to understand that this nutrition does not come from foods. Many of these products are very expensive as well. The whole scene is very unfortunate and requires a high level of education to sort out the truth.

Get professional guidance.

One last word to the wise. Standard Process and MediHerb supplements are not retail products. They are available through qualified, licensed healthcare professionals for a good reason: they require training. One must come to these two companies with a thorough understanding of the human body and appropriate clinical education.

I share this information in my book in hopes of reaching more people. Every single day I meet someone who hasn't heard of Standard Process or MediHerb. This reality both enlivens me and disappoints me. How can these people be unaware of these tools? These products are amazing, and I want to do my part to spread the good word.

That said, if you are interested, call Standard Process at 1-800-558-8740 to find a trained health professional near you.

Before I go, I want to leave you with a quote from Mark Anderson, an authority on Royal Lee's work:

"The Lee Principle of Nutrition states that a vitamin as it appears in nature is never a single chemical, but rather it is a group of interdependent compounds that form a 'nutrient complex' so intricate that only a living cell can create it. And just as no single component of a watch keeps time, no single compound in a vitamin complex accounts for the vitamin's nutritive effect in the body. Only through whole, unprocessed foods can the synergistic effect of a true vitamin be delivered."

MY LIBRARY

Welcome to my personal library.

Ever since I was 18 years old, books have been finding me. Reading has been a spiritual experience, each book arriving right on time to teach me what I needed to know to expand in my consciousness. I share my library with you because these books have created me, just like the food I eat.

Chapter 1: Eat in Peace

The Art & Science of Low Carbohydrate Living, by Volek and Phinney

The Big Fat Surprise, by Nina Teicholz

The Case Against Sugar, by Gary Taubes

Catching Fire: How Cooking Made Us Human, by Richard Wrangham

Cooked, by Michael Pollan

Coping with Food Intolerances, by Dick Thom

The Crazy Makers: How the Food Industry is Destroying Us, by Carol Simontacchi

Dealing with Food Allergies: A Practical Guide to Detecting Culprit Foods and Eating a Healthy, Enjoyable Diet, by Janice Vickerstaff Joneja

Defending Beef, by Hahn Niman

The Diabetes Solution, by Richard Bernstein

Diabetes and Hypoglycemia, by Michael Murray

The Diet Cure, by Julia Ross

Dr. Mandell's 5-Day Allergy Relief System, by Marshall Mandell and Lynne Scanlon

Eat Fat, Lose Fat: Three Delicious, Science-Based Coconut Diets, by Sally Fallon and Mary Enig

Encyclopedia of Natural Medicine, by Michael Murray and Joseph Pizzorno

Encyclopedia of Nutritional Supplements, by Michael Murray

Excitotoxins: The Taste that Kills, by Russell Blaylock

Fast Food Nation, by Eric Schlosser

Fat Flush Plan, by Ann Louise Gittleman

Fats that Heal and Fats that Kill, by Udo Erasmus

The Fourfold Path to Healing, by Tom Cowan

Get the Sugar Out, by Ann Louise Gittleman

A Grateful Heart: Daily Blessing for the Evening Meal from Buddha to the Beatles, by MJ Ryan

Grain Brain, by David Perlmutter

The Great Cholesterol Con, by Uffe Ravnskov

The Healing Nutrients Within, by Eric Braverman

The Healing Power of Minerals, by Paul Bergner

Healing with Whole Foods: Asian Traditions and Modern Nutrition, by Paul Pitchford

The Hungry Gene, by Ellen Ruppel Shell

Hypoglycemia for Dummies, by Chow and Chow

In Defense of Food, by Michael Pollan

Know Your Fats, by Mary Enig

Lick the Sugar Habit, by Nancy Appleton

Life Without Bread, by Allan and Lutz

The Maker's Diet, by Jordin Rubin

The Metabolic Typing Diet, by William Wolcott

The Miracle Cure of Stevia, by James A. May

The Mood Cure, by Julia Ross

The New Atkins for a New Year, by Eric Westman, et al.

The New Sugar Busters! Cut Sugar to Trim Fat, by Leighton Steward and Morrison Bethea

The No-Grain Diet, by Joseph Mercola

Nutritional & Physical Degeneration, by Weston A. Price

The Omnivore's Dilemma, by Michael Pollan

Potatoes not Prozac, by Kathleen DesMaisons

Primal Fat Burner: Live Longer, Slow Aging, Super-Power Your Brain, and Save Your Life with a High-Fat, Low-Carb Paleo Diet, by Nora Gedgaudas

Put Your Heart In Your Mouth, by Natasha Campbell McBride

Seeds of Deception, by Jeffrey Smith

Strong Medicine, by Blake Donaldson

Sugar Blues, by William Duffy

Sugar Busters! Cut the Sugar to Trim Fat, by Leighton Steward and Morrison Bethea

The Sugar Addict's Total Recovery Program, by Kathleen DesMaisons

The Sweetness and Power: The Place of Sugar in Modern History, by Sidney Mintz

Syndrome X: The Complete Nutritional Program to Prevent and Reverse Insulin Resistance, by Jack Challem and Burton Berkson

Traditional Foods Are Your Best Medicine, by Ron Schmid

Transformational Weight Loss, by Charles Eisenstein

The Vegetarian Myth, by Lierre Keith

The Untold Story of Milk, by Ron Schmid

Wheat Belly, by William Davis

The Whole Soy Story, by Kaayla Daniel

Why Am I Always So Tired?, by Anne Louise Gittleman

Why Can't I Lose Weight?, by Lorrie Medford

Why Do I Need Whole Food Supplements?, by Lorrie Medford

Why We Get Fat and What to do About It, by Gary Taubes

The Yoga of Eating, by Charles Eisenstein

Your Body Knows Best, by Ann Louise Gittleman

Cookbooks

Against All Grain, by Danielle Walker

Breaking the Vicious Cycle, by Elaine Gottschall

Ditch the Wheat, by Carol Lovett

Dr. Mercola's Total Health Cookbook and Program, by Joseph Mercola

Eat Like a Dinosaur, by The Paleo Parents

From Asparagus to Zucchini, by Madison Area Community Supported Agriculture Coalition

Full Moon Feast, by Jessica Prentice

The Grassfed Gourmet, by Shannon Hayes

Jack Allen's Kitchen, by Jack Gilmore

The Keto Diet: A Complete Guide to a High-Fat Diet, by Leanne Vogel

Make it Paleo, by Bill Staley and Hayley Mason

Nourishing Broth, by Sally Fallon

Nourishing Traditions, by Sally Fallon

The Nourishing Traditions Cookbook for Children, by Suzanne Gross and Sally Fallon

The Paleo Kitchen: Finding Primal Joy in Modern Cooking, by Juli Bauer and George Bryant

Paleo Soups and Stews, by Simone Miller

Primal Blueprint, by Mark Sisson

Wild Fermentation, by Sandor Katz

Chapter 2: Drink in Peace

Caffeinated: How Our Daily Habit Helps, Hurts, and Hooks Us, by Murray Carpenter

The Hidden Messages in Water, by Masaru Emoto

The Salt Fix: Why the Experts Got it All Wrong, by Dr James DiNicolantonio

Water for Health, for Healing, for Life, by Batmanghelidj

Your Body's Many Cries for Water, by Batmanghelidj

Chapter 3: Poop in Peace

The Body Ecology Diet: Recovering Your Health and Rebuilding Your Immunity, by Donna Gates

Clinical Purification, by Gina Nick

Digestive Wellness, by Elizabeth Lipski

Gut and Psychology Syndrome, by Natasha Campbell-McBride

Kiss Your Dentist Goodbye, by Ellie Phillips

The Second Brain, by Michael Gershon

What's Your Poo Telling You?, by Josh Richman

Herbal Medicine

Adaptogens: Herbs for Stress, Stamina, and Stress Relief, by David Winston and Steven Maimes

Adaptogens in Medical Herbalism, by Donald Yance

Between Heaven and Earth: A Guide to Chinese Medicine, by Harriet Beinfield and Efrem Korngold

The Big Herbs, by Paul Strauss

The Book of Herbal Wisdom: Using Plants as Medicine, by Matthew Wood

Botany in a Day, by Thomas Elpel

The Botany of Desire, by Michael Pollan

Chinese Herbal Medicine: Materia Medica, 3rd Edition, by Dan Bensky and Andrew Gamble

Clinical Applications of Ayurvedic and Chinese Herbs by Kerry Bone

Clinical Botanical Medicine, by Eric Yarnell and Cathy Abascal

A Clinical Guide to Blending Liquid Herbs, by Kerry Bone
The Consultation in Phytotherapy, by Peter Conway
The Constituents of Medicinal Plants, by Andrew Pengelly
The Dictionary of Modern Herbalism, by Simon Mills
Earthly Bodies and Heavenly Hair, by Dina Falconi
The Essential Book of Herbal Medicine, by Simon Mills
The Essential Guide to Herbal Safety, by Simon Mills and
    Kerry Bone
The Green Pharmacy, by James Duke
The Healing Power of Echinacea and Goldenseal, by Paul
    Bergner
The Healing Power of Ginseng, by Paul Bergner
Healthy Children: Optimising Children's Health with Herbs,
    by Rob Santich and Kerry Bone
Herbal Constituents, by Lisa Ganora
Herbal Manufacturing, by Jenny Adams and Eleanor Tan
Herbal Medicine from the Heart of the Earth, by Sharol Til-
    gner
Herbal Therapeutics, by David Winston
The Herbalist's Way, by Nancy and Michael Phillips
Herbs for Hepatitis C and the Liver, by Stephen Buhner
The Herbs of Life, by Lesley Tierra
The Lost Language of Plants, by Stephen Buhner
Los Remedios, by Michael Moore
The Magical Staff, by Matthew Wood
Making Plant Medicine, by Richo Cech
Medicinal Plants of the Desert and Canyon West, by Michael
    Moore
Medicinal Plants of the Mountain West, by Michael Moore

Medicinal Plants of the Pacific West, by Michael Moore

Medicinal Plants of Texas, by Nicole Telkes

Practical Wisdom in Natural Healing, by Deborah Frances

The Practice of Traditional Western Herbalism, by Matthew Wood

The Practicing Herbalist, by Margi Flint

Principles and Practice of Phytotherapy, 2nd edition, by Simon Mills and Kerry Bone

The Rhodiola Revolution, by Richard Brown and Patricia Gerbarg

Seven Herbs: Plants as Teachers, by Mathew Wood

The Ultimate Herbal Compendium, by Kerry Bone

The Way of Herbs, by Michael Tierra

The Web that has No Weaver, by Kaptchuk

Weeds Heal: A Working Herbal, by Isla Burgess

Why Do I Really Need Herbs?, by Lorrie Medford

The Wild Medicine Solution: Healing with Aromatic, Bitter, and Tonic Plants, by Guido Mase

The Yoga of Herbs, by David Frawley and Vasant Lad

Chapter 4: Rest in Peace

Dreamland: Adventures in the Strange Science of Sleep, by David Randall

Light's Out: Sleep, Sugar, and Survival, by T.S. Wiley

Sleepless in America: Is Your Child Misbehaving or Missing Sleep, by Mary Sheedy Kurcinka

Take a Nap, Change Your Life, by Sara Mednick

Chapter 5: Move in Peace

The Athlete Burnout Questionnaire Manual, by Thomas Raedeke and Alan Smith

Bikram's Beginning Yoga Class, by Bikram Choudhury

Dolphins and Their Power to Heal, by Amanda Cochrane and Karena Callen

Maps to Ecstasy: The Healing Power of Movement, by Gabrielle Roth

Move Your DNA, by Katy Bowman

The Sports Gene, by David Epstein

Chapter 6: Heal in Peace

Adrenal Fatigue: The 21st Century Stress Syndrome, by James Wilson

Breaking the Iron Triangle, by Robert Duggan

Energy: How it Affects Your Emotions, Your Level of Achievement, and Your Entire Personal Well Being, by Colin and Loren Chatsworth

From Fatigued to Fantastic, by Jacob Teitelbaum

The Last Well Person, by Norton Hadler

Maybe It Is All in Your Head . . . and You are Not Crazy, by Russell Roby

Medical Nemesis: The Expropriation of Health, by Ivan Illich

Surviving Mold: Life in the Era of Dangerous Buildings, by Ritchie Shoemaker

Tired of Being Tired, by Jesse Lynn Hanley and Nancy Deville

Vaccines and Autoimmunity, edited by Yehuda Shoenfield, et al.

What Happened, by Hillary Clinton

Why Can't I Get Better? Solving the Mystery of Lyme & Chronic Disease, by Richard Horowitz

Why Zebras Don't Get Ulcers: An Updated Guide to Stress, Stress-Related Diseases, and Coping, by Robert Sapolsky

Chapter 7: Live in Peace

Fertility/Pregnancy/Birthing/ Breastfeeding/Parenting

50 Human Studies Indicate Extreme Risk for Prenatal Ultrasound, by Jim West

The Aware Baby, by Aletha J. Solter

Bestfeeding: How to Breastfeed Your Baby, by Mary Renfrew, et al.

Birthing From Within, by Pam England & Rob Horowitz

Botanical Medicine for Women's Health, by Aviva Romm

Brilliant Babies, Powerful Adults: Awakening the Genius Within, by John Mike

Burning Woman, by Lucy Pearce

Calms: A Guide to Soothe Your Baby, by Debbie Takikawa and Carrie Contey

The Children of the Now, by Meg Blackburn Losey

The Conscious Parent, by Shefali Tsabary

The Continuum Concept, by Jean Leidloff

The Courage to Become: Stories of Hope for Navigating Love, Marriage and Motherhood, by Catia Hernandez Holm

The Family Bed, by Tine Thevenin

The Female Brain, by Louann Brizendine

The Garden of Fertility, by Katie Singer

The Greatest Experiment Ever Performed on Women, by Barbara Seaman

Keeping Your Child Healthy with Chinese Medicine, by Bob Flaws

Last Child in the Woods, by Richard Louv

The Magical Child, by Joseph Chilton Pearce

The Male Brain, by Louann Brizendine

Mind Over Labor, by Carl Jones

Mothering From Your Center, by Tami Lynn Kent

The Nourishing Traditions Book of Baby & Childcare, by Sally Fallon and Tom Cowan

Our Babies, Ourselves, by Meredith Small

The Oxytocin Factor, by Uvnas Moberg

The Pill, by Jane Bennett and AlexandraPope

Vaccination: Examining the Record, by Judith DeCava

What Mothers Do, Especially When it Looks like Nothing, by Naomi Stadlen

Wild Feminine, by Tami Lynn Kent

Wise Woman Herbal for the Childbearing Years, by Susun Weed

Women, Hormones, & the Menstrual Cycle, by Ruth Trickey

Your One-Year-Old, by Louise Ames (There is one book for each year of childhood. I recommend all of them.)

Addiction

Addiction & Grace: Love and Spirituality in the Healing of Addictions, by Gerald G. May

Alcoholics Anonymous, 3rd Edition

Alcoholism: The Cause and the Cure with the 101 Program, by Genita Petralli

Codependent's Guide to the Twelve Steps, by Melody Beattie

Courage to Change, by Al-Anon Family Groups

Seven Weeks to Sobriety: The Proven Program to Fight Alcoholism Through Nutrition, by Joan Matthews Larson

Nutrition and Addiction: A Plan for the Recovery from Addictive Disorders, by Gayle Hamilton and Nate Mayfield

One Day at a Time in Al-Anon (no author)

A Primer of Drug Action, by Robert Julien

The Relationship of Stress to Hypoglycemia and Alcoholism, by Jean Poulos

Twelve Steps and Twelve Traditions, by Alcoholics Anonymous

Your Drug May Be Your Problem: How and Why to Stop Taking Psychiatric Medications, by Peter Breggin and David Cohen

Self-Help/Personal Development

The Amazing Laws of Cosmic Mind Power, by Joseph Murphy

The Antidote: Happiness for People Who Can't Stand Positive Thinking, by Oliver Burkeman

The Art of Possibility, by Rosamund Stone Zander and Benjamin Zander

Better Than Before: Mastering the Habits of our Everyday Lives, by Gretchin Rubin

Big Magic, by Elizabeth Gilbert

Brave Enough, by Cheryl Strayed

Breaking the Grip of Dangerous Emotions, by Janet Maccaro

Crucial Conversations: Tools for Talking When the Stakes are High, by Kerry Patterson, et al.

Discover the Best in You, by Anne Gaylor

Don't Sweat the Small Stuff, and It's All Small Stuff, by Richard Carlson

Emotional Freedom: Liberate Yourself from Negative Emotions and Transform Your Life, by Judith Orloff

The Extraordinary Healing Power of Ordinary Things, by Larry Dossey

Find Your Courage: Unleash Your Full Potential and Live the Life You Really Want, by Margie Warrell

Flow: The Psychology of Optimal Experience, by Mihaly Csikszentmihalyi

Good Grief, by Mark Shearon

Happier, by Tal Ben-Shahar

Healing Trauma: A Pioneering Program for Restoring the Wisdom of Your Body, by Peter Levine

The Hidden Power, by Thomas Troward

How to Attract Money, by Joseph Murphy

How to Believe in Nothing and Set Yourself Free, by Michael Misita

How to Get What You Want and Want What You Have: A Practical and Spiritual Guide to Success, by John Gray

How to Win Friends and Influence People, by Dale Carnegie

The Language of Emotions, by Karla McLaren

Lean In, by Sheryl Sandberg

Life More Abundant, by Bill O'Hearn

Loving What Is, by Byron Katie

Making the Impossible Possible, by Jason Boreyko

Molecules of Emotion, by Candice Pert

The Nature Principle, by Richard Louv

Outliers: The Story of Success, by Malcolm Gladwell

Quiet, by Susan Cain

People of the Lie, by Scott Peck

The Power of Focus, by Jack Canfield and Mark Hansen

The Power of Your Spoken Word, by Florence Scovel Shinn

The Power of Your Subconscious Mind, by Joseph Murphy

Premeditated Success: Success Secrets of a Simple Minded Irishman, by Tom Murphy

Seven Secrets to Success: A Story of Hope, by Richard Webster

Special Meditations for Health, Wealth, Love, and Expression, by Joseph Murphy

Surviving Panic Disorder, by Stuart Shipko

Talk Like Ted, by Carmine Gallow

There Are No Accidents, by Robert Hopcke

There is Nothing Wrong with You, by Cheri Huber

There Once was a Tree called Deru, by Kakkib liDthia Warrawee

The Three Laws of Performance, by Steve Zaffron and Dave Logan

Think and Grow Rich, by Napoleon Hill

Thoughts are Things, by Bob Proctor

Tribes: We Need You to Lead Us, by Seth Godin

Turn the Page: How to Read like a Top Leader, by Chris Brady

Two, by Ralph Waldo Trine

Waking the Tiger: Healing Trauma, by Peter Levine

Way of the Peaceful Warrior: A Book that Changes Lives, by Dan Millman

What You Feel You Can Heal, by John Gray

You Already Know What to Do, by Sharon Franquemont

You Have the Power: Choosing Courage in a Culture of Fear, by Frances Moore Lappe

Your Sixth Sense, by Belleruth Naparstek

Your Word is Your Wand, by Florence Scovel Shinn

Relationships

Borderline Personality Disorder Demystified, by Robert Friedel

The Color Code: A New Way to See Yourself, Your Relationships, and Your Life, by Taylor Hartman

The Greatest Thing in the World—Love, by Henry Drummond

The Heart of the Soul, by Gary Zukav

The Highly Sensitive Person: How to Thrive When the World Overwhelms You, by Elaine Aron

Hold Me Tight: Seven Conversations for a Lifetime of Love, by Sue Johnson

How to Improve Your Marriage Without Talking About It, by Patricia Love

Men, Women and Relationships, by John Gray

Mastering Your Moods: Recognizing Your Emotional Style and Making It Work for You, by Melvyn Kinder

The Mastery of Love, by Don Miguel Ruiz

The Rules: Time-Tested Secrets for Capturing the Heart of Mr. Right, by Ellen Fein and Sherrie Schneider

Social Intelligence: The Revolutionary New Science of Human Relationships,

Wired for Love, by Stan Tatkin

Women Who Love Too Much, by Robin Norwood

Spirituality/Creativity

The Alchemist, by Paulo Coelho

Animal Speak, by Ted Andrews

Attunement: The Sacred Landscape - Exploring the Soul Through Radiant Healing, by Laurence Layne

The Biology of Belief, by Bruce Lipton

Conversations with God, Book 1, 2, and 3, by Neale Donald Walsch

Drops Like Stars, by Rob Bell

Eat, Pray, Love, by Elizabeth Gilbert

The Game of Life and How to Play It, by Florence Scovel Shinn

The Laws of Spirit, by Dan Millman

Love Wins, by Rob Bell

A New Earth, by Eckhart Tolle

The Road Less Traveled, by Scott Peck

Sex God, by Rob Bell

Spontaneous Evolution, by Bruce Lipton and Steve Bhaerman

Steal Like an Artist, by Austin Kleon

The Tao of Pooh, by Benjamin Hoff

The Tao of Abundance: Eight Ancient Principles for Abundant Living, by Laurence G. Boldt

The Te of Piglet, by Benjamin Hoff

When Things Fall Apart, by Pema Chodron

The World's Religions, by Huston Smith

Zen and the Art of Making a Living, by Laurence Boldt

Documentaries

Babies

Bought

The Business of Being Born

Cancer, Nutrition & Healing

Cereal Killers 1

Cereal Killers 2

Doctored

The Elegant Universe

Farmageddon

Fathead

Food Matters

The Future of Food

Genetic Roulette

Hungry for Change

In Utero
The Meaning of Tea
Moldy
My Big Fat Diet
Numen: The Nature of Plants
Orgasmic Birth
Pregnant in America
Prescription for Disaster
Rethinking Cancer
Take Back Your Power
The Sanctity of Sanctuary
The Secret
Statin Nation
That Sugar Film
Super Size Me
Sweet Misery: A Poisoned World
That Vitamin Movie
True Cost
Unrest
What Babies Want: An Exploration of the Consciousness of Infants
What the Bleep Do We Know!?

RECIPES

"Come eat with me, at the table of this life."
—KT TUNSTALL, SONG LYRICS
FROM *MADE OF GLASS*

A Word About Cooking
Breakfast
Main Dishes
Soups
Side Dishes
Salad Dressing
Snacks
Desserts
Beverages

A word about cooking

My husband and I watched an episode of *House of Cards* the other night in which four monks made an amazing piece of art with sand. It was a part of a peace-keeping ritual, I think. The monks spent days blowing colored sand into fabulous gorgeous shapes. When they were done with the design, they wiped it clean. They put the sand in a sacred jar. The art was gone.

Just. Like. That.

I thought to myself: that is like making a meal. Cooking is an act of love. It is making art that you eat. We create food and then it creates us.

I spend hours in my kitchen cooking for my family, not to mention all the time it takes to gather the ingredients. And for what? We sit down to eat, and poof, my creation is gone in ten minutes.

If I look at my time in the kitchen from that perspective, cooking sucks.

But the food's disappearance is an illusion.

Your work in the kitchen lives on—in you, and in your family. The food becomes you. You can see it in your glowing skin and bright eyes, and feel it in your clear mind. What you do in the kitchen radiates out into the entire world. It is where true, deep healing takes place and where we can maintain our sense of awe and wonder in the world. Whether you are transforming eggs and olive oil into homemade mayonnaise or vegetables into soup, cooking is transformative for the food and for our bodies.

So next time you are struggling in your kitchen cooking, wondering what's it all for . . . take a deep breath and think of me sitting on your shoulder, whispering into your ear: "Cooking matters."

But then picture me on your other shoulder, whispering into your other ear: "Sometimes cooking isn't the top priority."

When I've been too busy, or put out too much energy without downtime, my urge to be in the kitchen declines. Over the years, I've learned that this is ok! Instead of entering a spiral of shame, I purchase prepared food items and healthy convenience foods, knowing that at some point I will come back to my kitchen with JOY! I've learned to trust this natural flow of activity and rest. There's no need to force anything in your life.

And that includes forcing yourself to eat a specific way. You will find a variety of recipes offered here. That's by design. Your priorities may be different from someone else's. Maybe your first step is going gluten-free, or maybe you need to improve the quality of the carbohydrates you are eating. I respect your process and hope you enjoy the many gifts made with real food that come from my recipes.

By the way, I get a lot of questions about how people who have a dairy sensitivity can eat butter. It is because the immune system reacts to proteins, not fat, and there is very little protein in butter. On average a tablespoon of butter is 80% fat and the rest is mostly water with less than a gram of protein. So depending on the severity of your dairy sensitivity, you may (or may not be) fine with consuming butter. The purest form of butter is ghee, which has had the majority of proteins removed. Please know that in most of my recipes butter, ghee, and coconut oil are interchangeable, so I trust that you will find what works for your body.

Cook in peace!

Breakfast
ALMOND BUTTER BANANA PANCAKES
2 bananas
2 pastured eggs from Vital Farms
2 TBS almond butter

Combine with a hand mixer until smooth. Fry in coconut oil and lightly drizzle with maple syrup

PALEO PIGS IN A BLANKET

Fry sausage patties.

Combine in a small bowl:
2 ripe bananas
2 eggs
1 TSP vanilla extract

Mix with a hand mixer until smooth. Fry in coconut oil. Slice sausage patties and wrap in pancake. Drizzle with maple syrup.

PUMPKIN PANCAKES

1 cup almond flour
4 pastured eggs
½ cup organic canned pumpkin
2 TBS honey
1 TSP vanilla
¼ TSP sea salt
¼ TSP baking soda
¼ TSP cinnamon
¼ TSP cardamom
¼ TSP nutmeg

Mix all ingredients thoroughly in a bowl, and fry in coconut oil.

PUMPKIN PATCH WAFFLES

(From *Paleo Magazine*'s 3rd annual holiday cookbook–
Paleo, Primal & Grain-Free Recipes, by Trina Beck at
paelonewbie.com, pg. 20)

1 cup pumpkin purée
½ cup almond butter
1 TBS coconut flour
3 eggs, separated
1 TSP vanilla extract
1 TSP pumpkin spice
½ TSP baking soda
1 TBS maple syrup

Preheat waffle maker. Separate eggs, putting yolks in a
large bowl and whites in a small one. Beat egg whites until
stiff peaks form; set aside. Combine all the other ingredients in the large bowl with the egg yolks. Beat on low
speed for 3 minutes. It will be a thick batter. Then fold in
stiff egg whites. Cook in waffle maker. Serve with butter
and a touch of maple syrup.

BLUEBERRY LEMON PANCAKES

(Adapted from *The Paleo Kitchen,* by Juli Bauer and George Bryant, pg. 95)

3 eggs
½ cup, plus 3 TBS coconut milk
1 TBS honey
Juice from ½ lemon
Zest from a whole lemon
1 TSP vanilla
½ cup coconut flour
½ cup tapioca flour
½ TSP baking powder
½ TSP baking soda
Pinch of sea salt
Blueberries

In a large bowl, whisk the eggs and then add all of the wet ingredients. Whisk until combined. Add dry ingredients and whisk until smooth. Drop by spoonfuls onto a hot griddle smeared with coconut oil. Place a few blueberries on each pancake. Flip once and serve with butter and a touch of maple syrup.

PALEO HOT CEREAL

(Adapted from *Primal Blueprint, Quick and Easy Meals,* by Mark Sisson and Jennifer Meier, pg. 9)

½ cup walnuts
½ cup pecans
½–1 banana
¼ TSP cinnamon
¼ TSP vanilla bean powder
¼ TSP sea salt
¼ cup homemade nut milk or coconut milk
1–2 eggs

Add all ingredients to food processor and combine. Once blended, transfer to a pot and cook over medium heat, stirring frequently with a spatula. Serve with butter, maple syrup, and a splash of nut milk.

ALMOND FLOUR BISCUITS

2 ½ cups almond flour
½ TSP sea salt
½ TSP baking soda
½ cup butter (that's 1 stick, softened) or coconut oil
2 eggs
1 TBS honey

Preheat oven to 350 degrees. Combine dry ingredients in a medium-sized bowl. In a large bowl, combine wet ingredients. After the wet ingredients are blended, add the dry ones and stir gently until combined. For an artisan-style biscuit, drop by large spoonfuls onto a parchment-lined cookie sheet. Bake for 15–18 minutes, until browned on edges.

ZUCCHINI MUFFINS

(From *Breaking the Vicious Cycle*, by Elaine Gottschall, pg. 126)

3 cups nut flour
3 cups grated zucchini
5 TBS butter, melted
½ cup honey
3 eggs, beaten
1 TBS vanilla
2 TSP cinnamon
1 TSP baking soda
½ TSP sea salt

Preheat oven to 350 degrees. Combine the nut flour, zucchini, butter, and honey in a large bowl. Then, stir in beaten eggs, vanilla, cinnamon, baking soda, and sea salt. Pour into greased muffin pan. Bake for 18–20 minutes. Makes 1 dozen muffins.

NUT MUFFINS

1 ½ cups raw nuts
¼ cup maple syrup
3 eggs from pastured chickens
1 TSP vanilla extract
¼ TSP sea salt
Zest of 1 lemon or orange

Preheat oven to 375 degrees. Grind nuts to a powder in a Vitamix. Then add the rest of the ingredients and blend until smooth, scraping sides at least once. Pour into greased muffin pan. Bake for 10–12 minutes. Makes 6 muffins. Serve with butter. These will keep for 3 days in a tightly sealed container.

GLUTEN-FREE CINNAMON APPLE MUFFINS

1 cup almond flour
1 TBS arrowroot powder
2 eggs
3 TBS butter, melted
¼ cup maple syrup
1 apple, peeled, cored, and chopped
1 TSP vanilla
½ TSP cinnamon
¼ TSP sea salt
¼ TSP baking soda
¼ TSP baking powder

Preheat oven to 350 degrees. Combine all ingredients except apples in a small bowl. Blend well and then stir in the apples. Pour into a greased muffin tin. Bake for 12–15 minutes. Makes 6 muffins.

BLUEBERRY NUT MUFFINS
1 ½ cups almond flour
3 pastured eggs
¼ cup maple syrup
1 TSP vanilla extract
¼ TSP sea salt
½ cup blueberries

Preheat oven to 375 degrees. Combine all ingredients except blueberries in a small bowl and blend with a hand mixer until smooth. Then stir in blueberries and pour into a greased muffin tin. Bake for 15–20 minutes. Serve with butter. Makes 6 muffins.

EASY APPLE BERRY CRISP
(From *Paleo Magazine*, Oct/Nov 2015, pg. 95)

Preheat oven to 350 degrees.
Combine the following ingredients in a bowl:

4 medium apples, cored and cut into chunks
1 pint blueberries
1 TBS arrowroot
Juice of 1 lemon
1 TSP cinnamon
Pinch of sea salt

Toss all ingredients to combine thoroughly. Let it sit while you make the topping. Combine the following ingredients in a food processor until blended:

1 ½ cups almond flour
¾ cup walnuts
1 TSP cinnamon
Pinch of sea salt
¼ cup maple syrup
¼ cup butter (or coconut oil or ghee)

Stir the filling one more time and pour into a greased 9-inch pie or casserole dish. Sprinkle on topping and then cover with greased tin foil or a glass lid. Bake for 25 minutes. Remove the cover and continue baking for 20–25 minutes until golden brown.

BACON BERRY PEACH CRISP

Filling:
1 cup organic strawberries
1 cup organic blueberries
6–8 peaches
1 TBS vanilla extract
1 ½ TSP arrowroot powder

Topping:
½ cup walnuts or brazil nuts
½ cup pecans or hazelnuts
¼ cup date sugar
¼ cup oatmeal
¼ TSP cinnamon
¼ TSP cardamom
Pinch of sea salt
2–4 TBS butter
Bacon—enough to sprinkle on top

Cook the bacon, and set aside.

In a pot, combine fruit with vanilla extract. Cook on low for about 10 minutes, stirring frequently. Add arrowroot powder at the end to thicken the sauce.

In the meantime, put all of the topping ingredients except for the bacon into a food processor, and blend until combined.

Pour berries into a greased medium sized oven-safe dish; cover with topping. Break the bacon into small pieces and sprinkle on the topping, gently working it in so it's not sitting on top. Broil on low for about 5 minutes. Watch carefully; it has a tendency to cook fast and burn. Serve warm or cold. Top with coconut cream.

BERRY CRUMBLE
(Adapted from *Primal Blueprint*, by Mark Sisson and Jennifer Meier, pg. 5)

Filling:
3–4 cups of organic berries (frozen or fresh)*
1 TBS vanilla extract
1 TSP arrowroot powder

Topping:
½ cup walnuts or brazil nuts
½ cup pecans or hazelnuts
¼ cup date sugar**
¼ cup oatmeal**
¼ TSP cinnamon
¼ TSP cardamom
Pinch of sea salt
2–4 TBS butter

In a pot, combine berries with vanilla extract. Cook on low for about 10 minutes, stirring frequently. Add arrowroot powder to thicken.

In the meantime, put all of the topping ingredients into a food processor and blend until combined.

Pour berries into a greased medium sized oven-safe dish; cover with topping. Broil on low for about 5 minutes. Watch carefully; it has a tendency to cook fast and burn. Serve warm or cold.

*You can be very creative with this filling. Variations include pears, nectarines, peaches, and apples. All are delicious.

**If you are concerned about your carbohydrate intake, you can easily remove these two ingredients.

SOAKED OATS

(From *Nourishing Traditions*, by Sally Fallon with Mary G. Enig, Ph.D., pg. 455)

1 cup organic oats (steel cut or rolled, not quick-cooking)
1 cup filtered water
2 TBS apple cider vinegar or lemon juice
1 cup filtered water
1 TSP sea salt
Butter
Maple syrup
Blueberries or sliced bananas
Nuts
Flax seeds, ground

Soak oats in water and apple cider vinegar overnight in a tightly covered bowl, in a warm place. (If I do not have a lid, I use Saran Wrap, sealed with a rubber band, to cover the mixture.) The soaking process releases the nutrients. (For a more detailed discussion about this topic, refer to Sally Fallon's *Nourishing Traditions*.)

In the morning, bring additional water and sea salt to a boil; add oats and stir continuously. Turn heat down to low, stirring occasionally, until desired consistency is reached. Add a liberal amount of butter, and a touch of maple syrup for flavoring. Add fruit, nuts and/or flax seeds, if desired.

ALMOND FLOUR BANANA BREAD

1 ½ cups amond flour

4 eggs

¼ cup melted butter

½ cup maple sugar, xylitol or other dry natural sweetener

3 medium bananas, mashed (about ¾ cup banana puree)

1 TSP vanilla extract

¾ TSP cinnamon

½ TSP nutmeg

¾ TSP baking powder

½ TSP salt

½ cup walnuts (optional mix-in)

½ cup chocolate chips (optional mix-in)

Preheat oven to 350 degrees.

In a large bowl, mix together all ingredients except mix-ins, until there are not clumps. Fold in the walnuts, chocolate chips, or any other mix-ins you might want.

Lightly grease a 5" × 10" (or similar size) loaf pan and pour in the batter.

Bake for 45–55 minutes or until a cake tester inserted in the center comes out clean. Remove from oven and let cool completely before slicing.

LEMON POPPY SEED MUFFINS

2 cups finely ground almond flour
½ TSP salt
½ TSP baking soda
2 TBS poppy seeds
Zest of 1 lemon
1–2 TBS lemon juice
2 eggs
¼ cup butter (or oil of your choice)
¼ cup honey

Preheat oven to 350 degrees. Mix dry ingredients in a bowl. In a separate bowl, whisk together the wet ingredients. Combine wet and dry until well incorporated. Pour into lined muffin tins. Bake for 25–30 minutes (or until golden brown).

Main Dishes
SAUSAGE WITH POTATOES AND CABBAGE
(recipe by Jessica Prentice)

Bacon drippings, olive oil, or lard
2 leeks, thinly sliced, including much of the green part, or
1 large onion, sliced thin
1 head of cabbage, shredded
3 Yukon Gold potatoes, diced
Warm chicken broth (or water)
2 bunches of leafy greens, sliced into ribbons (I used broccoli greens, my new favorite)
½ TSP caraway seeds
4 whole sausages (I like Richardson's Farms Sweet Italian or Mulay's)
Sea salt and pepper to taste

Heat fat in a large pot and cook sausage. Once browned, add leeks. Once sausage is cooked, remove it from the pan and set aside. Add shredded cabbage to pan along with a pinch of salt and caraway seeds. Sauté until the cabbage begins to wilt. Add greens and stir gently. Add diced potatoes, another pinch of salt, and about ¼ cup warm broth. Cover, reduce heat and allow potatoes to steam until tender. Slice the sausage and add it back to the pan, stirring to incorporate and heat thoroughly. Add plenty of salt and black pepper to taste.

LEMON SAGE CHICKEN BREASTS

4–6 chicken breasts

Aloha Spice Seasoning for Chicken and Pork

8–12 slices of prosciutto, thinly sliced

Olive oil

Fresh sage

1–2 lemons

½ stick butter

1 TSP arrowroot powder

Preheat oven to 400 degrees. Pound chicken breasts with a mallet and then cut each breast in half. Season them with the spice seasoning and wrap each breast with a piece of prosciutto. Put olive oil in a large pan and cook chicken breasts over medium heat, about 3 minutes on each side. This usually takes 2 batches. Place the breasts on a large cookie sheet and bake for 10–12 minutes.

For the sauce, brown the butter until it smells nutty. Remove pan from heat and squeeze in the lemon juice and add the chopped sage. Whisk in the arrowroot powder to thicken, and then drizzle over the chicken breasts before serving.

CAJUN HONEY PORK TENDERLOIN

2–4 TBS butter

1–2 TBS honey

1–2 pork tenderloins

Cajun seasoning (I like Slap Ya Mama)

¾ cup water or chicken broth

1–3 TSP arrowroot powder

Fresh rosemary or chives, chopped

Preheat oven to 375 degrees. Using an oven-safe pot, heat butter and honey. Season tenderloin with Cajun spices. Then brown tenderloin for 5 minutes on each side, stirring frequently. Lower heat if honey burns. Place pot in oven and roast uncovered for 15–20 minutes. Combine arrowroot with water or broth and let it sit. When done, remove pork from pot and cover it with foil. Pour the broth preparation into the pot, along with rosemary or chives, and simmer for 5 minutes until thickened. Slice pork and drizzle liberally with sauce. Serve with lemon asparagus and potato slices.

BANGIN' LIVER
(By paleochef.com)

1 pound chicken liver, chopped (I got mine from Richardson's Farm at the Barton Creek Farmer's Market in Austin)
2 TBS pastured butter
3 TBS olive oil
6 garlic cloves, chopped
1 large green bell pepper, chopped
1 ½ TBS cumin powder (I grind the seeds in a coffee grinder for a robust flavor)
½ TSP ground cinnamon
¼ TSP ground ginger
¼ TSP ground cloves
¼ TSP ground cardamom
Dash of cayenne
Juice of 1 lemon
Sea salt

Heat butter and olive oil in a pan over low-medium heat. Chop chicken livers and sprinkle with salt. Gently add the liver to the pan and stir carefully until browned. Once browned, add the rest of the ingredients. Turn heat to low. Cover and cook for 15 minutes.

HERBED BUTTER FISH

2 filets of white fish
Jerk seasoning for seafood
Olive oil
1 shallot, diced
Kerrygold Garlic and Herb Butter
White wine

Heat olive oil on medium heat in frying pan. Add shallots and sauté until done. Season both sides of fish and add to the pan. Cook for a few minutes, and then add two pats of the herb butter. After the butter melts, give the pan a splash of white wine. Once you see white around the edges of the fish, flip it with a large spatula. Cook for a few more minutes. When done, gently slide the filets onto a serving plate and top with any remaining sauce.

MUSHROOM AND ONION CHICKEN
(From *Cooking Light*, March 2014)

4 chicken breasts (I like Smith & Smith and Dewberry Farms, if you live here in Austin)
Gluten-free flour (Bob's Redmill works just fine)
Seasoning for chicken (I like Aloha Spice for Chicken and Pork)
Olive oil
1 onion, sliced
8 ounces mushrooms, sliced
⅔ cup brandy
1 cup broth (chicken or beef; I like the beef bone broth from Vital Choice)
2 TSP arrowroot powder
1–2 TBS butter
Fresh thyme leaves

Heat 1 TBS of olive oil in a pan over medium heat. In the meantime, quickly cut chicken breasts in half and beat them with a mallet. Season them and dredge in flour. Fry them for about 2 minutes on each side, until done. You may need to do two batches; remember to add more oil. Remove from pan; set aside and keep warm.

While the chicken cooks, slice up the onion and mushrooms. Once the chicken is done, add another dash of olive oil to the pan and sauté the onions and mushrooms until browned. Stir frequently.

Combine broth and arrowroot in a large cup and whisk until smooth.

When onions are brown, take pan off the heat and add the brandy. Return to the stove and bring the mixture to a boil, cooking until almost all the liquid evaporates. Add the broth, stirring frequently. Add the chicken back to the pan, along with butter and fresh thyme.

Taste it before you serve to adjust for salt. I've made this recipe a hundred times, and the thicker your broth, the better it turns out.

GARLIC-STUFFED PORK TENDERLOIN
1–2 pounds pork tenderloin, pastured or at least organic
2–3 cloves of garlic, slivered vertically
Cajun seasoning (I like Slap Ya Mama)
Butter

Preheat oven to 350 degrees. Poke or stab small holes in the tenderloin with a sharp knife. Insert a sliver of garlic into each hole. Proceed to do this in an alternating fashion throughout the tenderloin. Season with Cajun seasoning; place small dabs of butter on top. Bake for 35–45 minutes, depending on size of tenderloin.

CHICKEN, RICE, AND VEGETABLES

1 pound chicken breast, pastured or at least organic

2 TBS olive oil

1 small onion, chopped

1 small green bell pepper, chopped

2–3 cloves garlic

1 can Rotel tomatoes with green chiles

1 ½ cup Texmati's light brown rice (or basmati rice)

1 ½ cups filtered water

2 chicken bouillon cubes (or Better than Bouillon, found at Whole Foods)

1 TSP sea salt

1 TSP pepper

1 TSP paprika

½ stick butter

Chop chicken into small pieces; sauté in olive oil over medium heat in a large saucepan (preferably one with a lid). Meanwhile, chop onion, bell pepper, and garlic; add when chicken is cooked. Stir in paprika, salt, and pepper. Add tomatoes to chicken and vegetables. Fill empty Rotel can with water and stir in, along with bouillon cubes. Bring to a boil, and add rice. Cover and cook for 25–30 minutes, until liquid is dissolved. Turn off heat, uncover, and let sit for 2 minutes; stir in butter and let sit for another 3 minutes.

SALMON CAKES

1 can wild Alaskan salmon (www.vitalchoice.com)
1 egg from pastured chicken
2–3 green onions, chopped
Salmon seasoning
Gluten-free breadcrumbs
1 TBS olive oil
1 TBS butter
Lemon wedges

Combine first five ingredients in a bowl and form into small patties. Cook over medium heat in a frying pan, using a combination of olive oil and butter; brown on both sides. Serve with lemon wedges.

STEAK SMOTHERED IN ONIONS

2 TBS olive oil
1 ½ pounds beef round cube steak
Steak seasoning
½ cup gluten-free flour
3 onions, sliced
Filtered water or broth

Place olive oil in a large skillet over medium-high heat.
Slice steaks in to an appropriate size (3" by 3" or so). Season
steaks and dredge in flour. Place in pan and sear on both
sides until browned. Smother steaks with sliced onions.
Add enough water to cover the meat. Cover and reduce
heat to medium-low. Simmer for one hour, stirring occasionally. The water and onions will form a nice gravy. If it
appears too thin, sprinkle additional flour into the pan and
continue to cook on low to thicken. Season to taste before
serving.

VEGETABLE MEAT LOAF

(*Breaking the Vicious Cycle,* by Elaine Gottschall, pg. 118)

1 ½ pounds grass-fed ground beef
1 egg
1 medium fresh tomato or ½ cup tomato juice
1 medium onion, cut in pieces
Sprig of parsley
1 stalk of celery, cut in pieces
Small amount of green pepper, cut up
1 carrot, cut in pieces

Place tomato or tomato juice into blender first. Push down on tomato to release juices so that blender blades will turn easily. Add egg and blend for a few seconds. Add remaining vegetables and blend until fairly smooth. Empty blender contents into bowl and mix well with the ground beef. Season with salt and pepper. Form mixture into a loaf and place in a shallow pan. Spread top with organic ketchup and dried parsley. Bake at 350 degrees for about 1 hour.

ROASTED STICKY CHICKEN

(*The Sugar Addict's Total Recovery Program,* by Kathleen DesMaisons, pg. 230)

1 large roasting chicken, pastured or at least organic
Olive oil
4 TSP sea salt
2 TSP paprika
1 TSP cayenne
1 TSP onion powder
1 TSP thyme
1 TSP white pepper
½ TSP garlic powder
½ TSP black pepper
1 chopped onion
1–2 cloves garlic, crushed

Combine seasonings in a small bowl.

Remove giblets from chicken cavity. Thoroughly rinse the chicken and dry it with paper towels. Rub the chicken with 1–2 tablespoons olive oil (this allows the seasoning to stick better). Cover the chicken evenly inside and out with the seasoning, and stuff it with the onion and garlic. Place in a baking pan and cover with Saran Wrap; let marinate overnight in the refrigerator.

Preheat oven to 250 degrees and bake chicken for 5 hours. After the first hour or so, baste the chicken every half hour. Let the chicken rest for 10 minutes before carving.

SPAGHETTI AND MEATBALLS*

1 pound grass-fed ground beef
1 pound pastured ground pork
1 egg
½ cup gluten-free bread crumbs
Seasonings: Herbes de Provence, sea salt, black and red pepper
2 TBS olive oil
1 large onion, diced
5 cloves garlic, diced
4 ribs of celery, diced
1 green bell pepper, diced
1 red, orange, or yellow bell pepper, diced
1 large can organic whole tomatoes (Muir Glen)
1 large can organic crushed tomatoes (Muir Glen)
1 small can organic tomato paste
Seasonings: Herbes de Provence, basil, thyme, sage, paprika, parsley, sea salt, black and red pepper

Preheat oven to 350 degrees. To make meatballs, combine beef, pork, egg, breadcrumbs, and seasonings in a large bowl; do not over mix. Form into one and a half-inch diameter balls. Place on cookie sheet; bake for 20–25 minutes.

Meanwhile, prepare sauce. Heat olive oil in a large pot. Sauté onion, garlic, and celery until desired tenderness; add bell peppers. Add whole and crushed tomatoes, along with tomato paste. Fill empty tomato paste can with filtered water and pour in to provide additional liquid. Stir; add seasonings. Simmer on low heat, covered, for 30 minutes. Add meatballs; simmer another 30 minutes.

Serve over zucchini noodles, brown rice pasta, or almond flour pasta. Can easily freeze extra sauce for future use.

*If time is limited, you can bypass making the meatballs and instead cook beef and pork in the large soup pot; set aside in a bowl and follow the directions for making the sauce, adding the meat back at the end.

Soups

FOR THE STOCK:

Put a whole chicken (local and organic is ideal) in a stock-pot full of water. Bring it to a boil and then let it simmer for 1.5–2 hours, until the chicken falls apart. Once the chicken is cooked, use a strainer with a long handle to remove the chicken, and place in a bowl to cool. Once it's cool enough to handle, pull the chicken off the bones and store in the fridge.

Now add a chopped onion, 3–4 roughly chopped carrots, and 6 ribs of coarsely chopped celery to the broth. Bring to a boil again and then turn down heat to simmer. Once the vegetables are limp and lifeless, usually a few more hours, strain the broth into another pot and discard the vegetables. To give you an idea of the total time, I started at 1:30 and was done at 8:30 in the evening. You will need to add water throughout the cooking process, as it will evaporate.

FOR THE SOUP:

4 finely chopped carrots
4 finely chopped ribs of celery
½ onion, chopped
3 cloves of garlic, minced
2 TBS olive oil

Sauté vegetables in olive oil in a large pot. Once tender, add the shredded chicken, along with enough broth to fill the pot (you'll still have some chicken and broth left over to freeze). Bring soup to a boil and then turn down heat to a simmer; season with sea salt and pepper to taste. Finish it off with freshly chopped parsley.

RUSTIC VEGETABLE SOUP

3–4 TBS extra-virgin, cold-pressed, unrefined olive oil
2 medium onions, diced
2–3 celery ribs, diced
2 sweet potatoes, peeled and chopped into small squares
3 cups vegetable or chicken broth
2 TSP paprika
1 TSP turmeric
1 TSP dried basil
1 bay leaf
1 TSP sea salt
Dash of cinnamon
Dash of cayenne
2 medium-sized tomatoes, diced
1 red bell pepper, diced
1 can cooked chickpeas, rinsed and drained
1 TBS tamari
2 garlic cloves, diced

In a soup kettle or extra large saucepan, sauté onions, celery, and sweet potatoes in olive oil. Add seasonings and broth. Simmer uncovered for 15 minutes. Add tomatoes, bell pepper, chickpeas, and tamari. Simmer another 10 minutes or until vegetables reached desired tenderness. Add garlic immediately before serving.

Note: The vegetables in this soup are flexible, so be creative! Any orange vegetable can be combined with a green one. Peas or green beans can replace the bell pepper, and carrots or winter squash can replace the sweet potatoes.

ASPARAGUS SOUP
(from Karen Murray with Eddison and Melrose Catering)

3 pounds asparagus
3 leeks, white part only, cleaned and sliced
2 TBS butter or olive oil
6 cups chicken or vegetable stock
Juice of one lemon
Sea salt and black pepper, to taste
Minced parsley

Prepare asparagus: remove ends. Cut 1 inch from the asparagus tips, slice diagonally into thin slivers, and reserve. Cut the remaining asparagus into 1-inch lengths, and set aside.

In a heavy-bottomed stockpot, melt butter or olive oil over medium heat. Add leeks and cook until translucent, about 5 minutes.

Add the asparagus pieces (not the tips) and the stock. Bring to a boil over high heat, reduce, and simmer until asparagus is tender, about 10 minutes.

Remove from heat and cool slightly. Puree mixture with a hand blender or in small batches in a blender. Add lemon juice and season with salt and pepper.

To serve, bring soup to a simmer, and add the reserved asparagus tips. Cook 2 to 3 minutes until tips are softened. Serve soup topped with a sprinkling of minced parsley.

CLEANSING SOUP
3 cups filtered water
1 TBS freshly grated ginger root
1–2 TBS miso paste (South River Miso Company)
1–2 green onions, chopped
1–2 TBS cilantro, chopped
1 TBS kelp flakes, optional (www.ryandrum.com)
1–2 pinches cayenne pepper
1 TBS olive oil
Juice of half a lemon

Boil water in a small pot; add ginger and simmer on low for 10 minutes. Turn off heat; stir in miso paste until dissolved. Add green onions, cilantro, kelp, cayenne, olive oil, and lemon juice. Cover and steep for 10 more minutes.

Side Dishes
LEAFY GREENS
3 slices of bacon

2 bunches of leafy greens (My favorite combination is collard greens and dandelion leaves. No matter how much I want to like kale, we just don't get along.)

½ to 1 cup homemade chicken broth

Juice of 1 lemon

1 garlic clove, diced

Dice bacon and cook over medium heat in a large pan. While it's cooking, remove stems from the greens and tear the leaves into pieces. When the bacon is done, add greens and then pour in the broth. Cover the pan with a lid to steam the greens, stirring often. When desired texture is achieved, squeeze a lemon over the greens and add garlic. Serve with your favorite protein.

OKRA AND TOMATOES
½ pound bacon, diced

1 onion, diced

1–2 cloves garlic, diced

1 pound okra, sliced into ½-inch pieces

2–3 tomatoes, diced

Sea salt, if needed

Black and red pepper

Cook bacon in a medium-sized pot over medium heat. When bacon is cooked, add onion and garlic; sauté until translucent. Add okra and cook until slimy, stirring often (do not leave unattended, the okra will stick to the bottom of the pan very quickly). After the okra becomes slimy, add tomatoes. Continue to cook on low uncovered until the okra has reached desired texture, stirring often. If the okra appears dry, then add more tomatoes, fresh or canned. Add seasonings when okra is finished cooking. This dish reheats well, but you may need to add a little water.

HERBED CAULIFLOWER RICE
1 head of cauliflower
Olive oil
½ onion, chopped
1 clove garlic, chopped
Salt, pepper, and dried parsley

Cut cauliflower in half and break off florets. Place them in small batches in a food processor and pulse until coarsely ground. Put olive oil in a large pan over medium heat and sauté onion and garlic. Then add the cauliflower, stirring frequently with a spatula. Season to taste with salt, pepper, and parsley.

GOLDEN MASHED POTATOES

Bake 1–2 sweet potatoes in the oven. I wrap mine in tinfoil and bake at 400 degrees until soft.

Then, boil 6–8 red-skinned potatoes in a pot with 4 cloves garlic. This usually takes 20–25 minutes, depending on the size of the potatoes. Poke the potatoes with a fork to assess the situation. You will know they're done when your fork slides in easily.

Strain the water from the pot, using the lid to hold back the potatoes. Take the skins off the sweet potatoes and add to the boiled potatoes, along with:

½ stick butter
Dash of garlic powder
Several dashes of dried parsley

Salt and pepper to taste. Beat with a hand mixer until smooth. Serve with bacon pieces sprinkled on top.

CAULIFLOWER MASHERS

1 head of cauliflower
½ stick butter
1 TSP sea salt

Cut cauliflower into chunks. Steam for 10 minutes. Strain. Add cauliflower to blender with butter and salt. Blend until smooth.

SOUTHERN CORNBREAD DRESSING

2 cups heirloom cornmeal (I get mine from Richardson Farms at the Barton Creek Farmer's Market in Austin)

1 cup water

¼ cup honey

5 TBS butter

5 TSP baking powder

½ TSP sea salt

Preheat oven to 400 degrees. Grease a small iron skillet. Combine all ingredients in a large bowl and stir until smooth. Pour into skillet. Bake for 20–25 minutes.

Gluten-free bread and cornbread (above), cubed and dried

1 pound grass-fed ground beef (Chickamaw Farms)

1 pound pork sausage (Richardson Farms or Mulays)

1 bell pepper

1 onion

6 ribs of celery, with leaves

1 bunch green onions

Fresh sage

Cajun seasoning (I like Slap Ya Mama)

Homemade chicken broth or turkey drippings

Preheat oven to 350 degrees. Grease a 9" by 13" pan with butter or lard. Cook beef and sausage in a pan. Coarsely chop the bell pepper, onion, celery, and green onion and combine with dried bread in a large bowl. Then mix in the fully cooked meat. Add broth to moisten. Place in greased pan. If it still looks dry, add more broth or drippings. Bake for an hour or more. You might need to increase oven temperature to 400 degrees for the last 10 minutes to brown. Serve hot with gravy.

CABBAGE

1 head organic cabbage
2–4 strips of bacon
½ onion
1–3 TBS broth or water

Dice bacon and cook it in a pot. Meanwhile, chop the onion and shred the cabbage: just cut it in half and quarter it, cutting the stalk out. Slice thin. The thinner you slice it, the faster it will cook. Once bacon is done, sauté onions and then add the cabbage. Stir frequently and put a lid on it to speed things up. You may need to add some of the liquid suggested above, if it looks dry. Cook until tender.

SWEET POTATO BAKE

Wrap 3–4 sweet potatoes in tin foil. Bake at 400 degrees from 1 to 1 ½ hours, depending on their size.

In the meantime, combine the following ingredients in a large bowl:

½ stick butter
¼ cup maple syrup
¼ cup cashew cream
¼ TSP sea salt
1 TSP cinnamon

Once the sweet potatoes are done, let cool and then scoop out the flesh. Mix well with a hand mixer and pour into a buttered 8" by 8" glass dish. Preheat the oven to 350 degrees.

Now make the topping. Place all of the following ingredients in a food processor:

½ cup walnuts
½ cup pecans
Pinch of sea salt
¼ TSP cinnamon
¼ TSP cardamom
1 TBS butter
¼ cup gluten-free oatmeal
¼ cup date sugar or 4–6 fresh dates

Blend until smooth. Then dribble on top of sweet potatoes. Bake covered for 30 minutes, and then uncovered for another 20–30 minutes. Serve warm. If your diet is restricted, you may eliminate the oatmeal and dates.

DIRTY RICE

Cook rice according to package directions.

1 pound pork sausage (Richardson Farms or Mulays)
1 pound grass-fed ground beef
½ green bell pepper
½ red bell pepper
3–4 ribs of celery
1 small onion
Cajun seasoning (I like Slap Ya Mama)
1 bunch green onions, sliced

Cook the meat in a large pot in a bit of olive oil. I like to mash it with a potato masher as it cooks to get a consistent look to the meat. Meanwhile, chop all the veggies and add them to the cooked meat, along with the rice. Stir until well combined and top with fresh green onions.

TAHINI ROASTED CAULIFLOWER
(Adapted from *Cooking Light*, March 2015, myrecipes.com)

Preheat oven to 475 degrees.

With a whisk in a large bowl combine:
⅓ cup tahini
2 TBS extra-virgin olive oil (or coconut oil)
1–2 TSP seasoning of your choice (I like Mt. Elbert All-Purpose Seasoning from Savory Spice Shop)

Add small florets from one head of organic cauliflower, and toss to coat.

Arrange cauliflower florets in a single layer on a lightly oiled baking sheet.

Roast 15 minutes, stirring halfway through.

Remove from oven and squeeze the juice of one lemon over top. Sprinkle with fresh or dried parsley. Serve immediately (this is a good leftover as well, particularly if you need extra vegetables for a quiche).

LAURI'S FAVORITE WINTER SALAD WITH CREAMY TAHINI DRESSING

(Adapted from *A Guide to Cooking Farm-Fresh Seasonal Produce: From Asparagus to Zucchini,* by Madison Area Community Supported Agriculture Coalition, pg. 184)

1 beet
2–3 carrots
¼ to ½ red cabbage
1 zucchini
1 yellow squash
1 red onion
1 fennel bulb
1 bunch parsley

Grate the beets, carrots, cabbage, zucchini, and squash into a large bowl. Finely chop onion, fennel, and parsley. Mix all the vegetables together. Note that the type and amount of vegetables can be easily altered. Serve with the following salad dressing.

Salad Dressings
CREAMY TAHINI DRESSING
(Adapted from *A Guide to Cooking Farm-Fresh Seasonal Produce: From Asparagus to Zucchini*, by Madison Area Community Supported Agriculture Coalition, pg. 184)

3 TBS sesame seeds
½ cup tahini
¼ cup lemon juice
¼ cup sesame oil
¼ cup olive oil
¼ cup tamari
Pinch of cayenne
1 TSP dried dill weed

Combine all ingredients in a jar and stir/shake well. If too thick, add a bit of water to thin it out.

MAPLE VINAIGRETTE SALAD DRESSING

1 shallot, quartered
½ cup apple cider vinegar
1 cup maple syrup
1 TSP sea salt
½ TSP black pepper
2 ½ cups olive oil

Place the first five ingredients in a blender; blend until smooth. With the blender running on its lowest speed, slowly pour in olive oil in a steady stream, until combined.

BALSAMIC HERB SALAD DRESSING

Handful of fresh herbs: basil, sage, tarragon, rosemary, marjoram, thyme, etc.
¼ cup organic balsamic vinegar
¼ cup raw apple cider vinegar
Juice of 1 lemon
2 cloves garlic
1 TSP dried mustard
½ to 1 TSP raw honey
Dash of sea salt and pepper
1 cup organic, extra-virgin, unrefined olive oil

Place all ingredients except oil in a blender; mix until combined. With blender running on medium speed, slowly pour oil in a steady stream until emulsified. Store in a glass jar in refrigerator. It will harden, so set out for 10–15 minutes before serving and shake well. Serve lightly drizzled over salad greens.

MAYONNAISE

3 eggs
1 ¼ TSP dry mustard
1 ½ TSP sea salt
¼ cup lemon juice
1 garlic clove (optional)
1 ¼ cup olive oil

Blend everything in a Vitamix, except the olive oil. Quickly increase speed to high and then slowly pour in the olive oil in a steady, smooth stream. Takes about 60 seconds to thicken. Refrigerate in a glass container. Will keep for 2–4 weeks.

CREAMY MAPLE SALAD DRESSING

1 cup homemade mayonnaise
¼ cup real maple syrup
¼ cup of your favorite vinegar

Combine all ingredients in blender and enjoy on your favorite salad.

PALEO RANCH DRESSING

(*A Year of Seasonal Menu Plans,* by Amanda Love at www. thebarefootcook.com)

1 cup mayonnaise
¼ cup full-fat coconut milk
2 TBS lemon juice
3 TBS minced fresh herbs (dill, chives, parsley)
1 clove garlic, minced
¼ TSP sea salt
Freshly cracked pepper, to taste

Whisk all the ingredients in a small bowl until smooth. So easy, so delicious. I rarely have all the fresh herbs, but dried works just as well.

PALEO AVOCADO RANCH DRESSING

(*A Year of Seasonal Menu Plans,* by Amanda Love at
www.thebarefootcook.com)

½ cup homemade mayonnaise
½ cup full-fat coconut milk
1 avocado, mashed
2 TBS lemon juice
3 TBS fresh or dried herbs (dill, chives, or parsley)
1 clove of garlic
¼ TSP sea salt
Cracked black pepper to taste

Combine all ingredients in a small bowl and whisk until
combined. Store in fridge.

Snacks

DEVILED EGGS

(Adapted from *Jack Allen's Kitchen*, by Jack Gilmore and Jessica Dupuy, pg. 116)

1 dozen eggs
4 TBS homemade mayonnaise
1 TBS apple cider vinegar
1 TBS mustard (you can use up to 2 TBS of Dijon, if you like)
4 TBS green onion, minced
2 TBS red bell pepper, minced
2 TBS parsley, minced
4 slices of bacon, chopped
1–2 dill pickles, chopped, optional (I love Pogue Mahone, available here in Austin)
Sea salt and pepper, to taste

Put the eggs in a large pot and thoroughly cover with water. Bring to a boil and then turn off the heat and let sit for 10 minutes. Put the eggs in a large bowl with water and ice and refrigerate for an hour or so. Gently crack the shells and run cool water over the eggs while you peel them. Cut eggs in half lengthwise and put yolks in a large bowl combined with all ingredients. Mash it all up with a fork and then fill egg cavities. Sprinkle with a dash of dried parsley and paprika.

HERBAL JELLO

2 cups fresh-squeezed orange juice

4 scoops Vital Proteins

2 TBS honey

1 TBS liquid herbs (I like the glycetracts from Mediherb: Echinacea Purpurea 1:3, Marshmallow root 1:5, and Chamomile 1:2, which is a water/alcohol extract)

Combine the orange juice and gelatin in a pot. Stir until combined and let sit for 5 minutes. Over medium heat, stir constantly until smooth. Then stir in honey and herbal extracts. Pour into a glass pan. Refrigerate until set.

Desserts
VANILLA CHIA PUDDING
2 small cans coconut cream
Homemade nut milk
1 TBS vanilla extract
1 TSP vanilla bean powder
10 drops stevia liquid extract
Pinch of sea salt
½ cup chia seeds

When measuring out the homemade nut milk, just fill each empty can of coconut cream with the milk, essentially giving you 4 cans of milk. Place all ingredients, except chia seeds, in blender and blend thoroughly. Place chia seeds in a large bowl, and pour the milk mixture over them; stir well and place in fridge.

Remember to stir at least once more before it sets to keep the seeds from clumping. You can have fun with the ingredients, adding cinnamon, cardamom, ginger, cloves, or whatever spices you like—even orange zest would be nice.

You can also add 2 TBS of cocoa or matcha for different flavors.

COCONUT WHIPPED CREAM

2 cans of organic coconut cream, refrigerated

1 TBS maple syrup

1 TSP vanilla

¼ TSP cinnamon

Open the cans from the bottom and pour off the liquid. Scoop the cream out into a small bowl and add the other ingredients. Whip it on high with a hand mixer.

Please see my online videos at charlottekikel.com for a cooking demonstration on how to make coconut whipped cream.

"GET SOME" ICE CREAM
(From www.bulletproofexec.com)

Combine the following ingredients in blender and blend until smooth. Then freeze in your ice cream maker.

4 eggs (pastured)
4 egg yolks
1 TSP vanilla bean powder
Juice from ½ lemon or 10 drops ACV
7 TBS grass fed butter (pastured)
7 TBS coconut oil
3 TBS + 2 TSPS MCT oil
5 TBS xylitol

I have made many fun variations of this ice cream.

Green Tea: add 1 TBS organic matcha.

Mexican Chocolate: ⅓ cup cocoa powder and 1 TSP organic cinnamon.

Chocolate Chip Cookie Dough: add chunks of Cappello's Chocolate Chip cookie dough to the ice cream maker when the ice cream is almost frozen.

Peppermint Patty: Find a healthy peppermint patty option. I get some from Trader Joe's that only have three ingredients: honey, chocolate and mint. Put the bag in the freezer beforehand, chop up four to six patties, and then add to the ice cream while it is freezing in the ice cream maker.

You can also make a root beer float with the vanilla ice cream and Live Soda Kombucha Root Beer, or a Dreamsicle float with vanilla ice cream and Live Soda Kombucha Dreamy Orange. Both are an outstanding way to cool off in the summer months.

HARVEST PIE

1 cup each: dried apricots, prunes, cranberries
½ cup raisins
½ cup goji berries
2 cups chopped apples and pears
½ cup chopped walnuts
4 TBS butter
2 TSP pumpkin pie spice
Pinch of salt

Cut apricots and prunes into bite size pieces and put in a large pot. Add all remaining fruit and the apple juice and simmer on low for about 15 minutes. You might need to add a bit of arrowroot to thicken. Remove from heat and cool. Stir in butter, spices and salt. Pour into a nut-based piecrust (see below for crust recipe). Refrigerate. Serve with coconut whipped cream (how-to video is available on my website charlottekikel.com).

CASHEW "CHEESECAKE"

For crust:

Combine all ingredients in food processor until blended, then press into an 8-inch springform pan:

½ cup raw pecans
½ cup pitted dates
¼ cup shredded coconut
2 TBS butter or coconut oil
Pinch of sea salt

For filling*:

Combine all ingredients in a Vitamix until smooth. Then pour into crust. Freeze for 4 hours to set and then move to refrigerator.

3 ½ cups cashews that have been soaked overnight in water (this is an important step that releases the nutrition of the cashews)
⅔ cup maple syrup
⅔ cup coconut oil, gently melted
⅔ cup fresh lemon juice
1–2 TSPS vanilla extract or crushed vanilla beans
Zest of 1 lemon (optional, for a more lemon flavor)

For raspberry topping:
Combine all ingredients in a Magic Bullet until smooth and then drizzle on your "cheesecake" upon serving:

½ cup raspberries
¼ cup water
1 TSP honey
1 TSP vanilla extract
1 TSP nut milk

*I have made many variations of this cheesecake, which include:

Lemon Green Tea: use zest of 1 lemon and add 1 TBS organic matcha.

Raspberry Lime: add ½ cup fresh raspberries to the filling, use lime juice instead of lemon juice, and add zest of one lime to the raspberry sauce.

Pumpkin Cinnamon: add 1 cup organic canned pumpkin to the filling, along with 1–2 TBS pumpkin pie spice (use more for a robust flavor).

Orange Dreamsicle: add 1 additional TSP of vanilla bean powder and the zest of one orange to the filling, and use orange juice instead of lemon juice.

GLUTEN-FREE OATMEAL COOKIES

1 ½ cups gluten-free oats

1 ½ cups almond flour

½ TSP sea salt

½ TSP baking soda

1 TBS cinnamon

2 TBS freshly ground flax seed

¼ cup maple syrup

¼ cup honey

¼ cup coconut oil

¼ cup butter, softened

1 egg

1 TBS vanilla

2 cups of add-ins (dark chocolate chips, raisins, chopped nuts, coconut, cranberries, etc.)

Preheat oven to 350 degrees. Combine dry ingredients in a large bowl. Add the wet ingredients and mix well. Drop by spoonful on a parchment-lined baking sheet and bake. I like them a little under-cooked, about 8–10 minutes, depending on their size.

GLUTEN-FREE GINGER SNAPS
(Adapted from *Nourishing Traditions*, by Sally Fallon with Mary G. Enig, pg. 530)

1 ½ cups almond flour
½ cup butter or coconut oil
1 cup arrowroot
½ cup maple sugar
1 TBS vanilla extract
1 ½ TSP ground ginger
1 TSP cinnamon
¼ TSP nutmeg
¼ TSP ground cloves
½ TSP sea salt

Preheat oven to 300 degrees. Place all ingredients in food processor and blend well. Form into small balls, place on a parchment-lined cookie sheet, and bake for 5 minutes. Then, remove from oven and press each cookie with the tines of a fork. Return to oven and continue baking for another 10–15 minutes, until done.

PUMPKIN CRUMBLE BARS
(*Paleo Magazine*, Oct/Nov 2015, pg. 98)

In a large bowl, whisk together:

½ cup creamy almond butter
½ cup pumpkin puree
⅓ cup maple syrup
2 large eggs, slightly beaten

Then add and whisk to combine:

2 TSP cinnamon
½ TSP ground ginger
¼ TSP ground or freshly ground nutmeg
½ TSP baking soda
Pinch of sea salt

Preheat oven to 350 degrees. Pour mixture into an 8" by 8" glass pan smeared with coconut oil.

For topping*, combine all ingredients in food processor until smooth:

½ cup pecans
⅓ cup almond flour
½ TSP ground cinnamon
Pinch of sea salt
1 TBS maple syrup
1 TBS coconut oil or butter

Sprinkle the topping onto the batter and bake for 25 minutes, or until firm to the touch.

*You can make these even more wonderful by sprinkling dark chocolate chunks on top.

GRAINLESS GRANOLA BALLS
(From *Paleo Magazine*, Aug/Sept 2015, pg. 98)

½ cup raw pecans
½ cup raw pumpkin seeds
½ cup almond flour
1 TSP cinnamon
½ TSP sea salt
1 cup raw walnuts, chopped
¼ cup dried cranberries, chopped
¼ cup dark chocolate mini chips
¼ cup honey
2 TBS almond butter
1 TBS vanilla

Preheat oven to 350 degrees. In a food processor, combine the pecans, pumpkin seeds, almond flour, cinnamon, and salt. Pulse until a coarse meal forms, and thentransfer to a medium-sized bowl. Stir in the walnuts, dried cranberries, and chocolate chips. Then add honey, almond butter, and vanilla. Stir gently to combine. This will make a thick dough. Form into balls, place on cookie sheet, and bake for 20–22 minutes.

NUTTY BLUEBERRY PROTEIN BALLS

(From *Primal Blueprint*, by Mark Sisson and Jennifer Meier, pg. 3)

4 pitted dates
1 cup raw walnuts
½ cup raw macadamia nuts
2 TBS coconut oil
¼ cup coconut flakes
½ cup blueberries

Place dates in food processor and blend until a paste forms. Add walnuts and macadamia nuts and blend until finely chopped. Slowly pour in coconut oil, until just combined. Place mixture in a bowl and gently stir in coconut flakes and blueberries. Roll into small balls and dredge in more shredded coconut. Store in refrigerator.

HOMEMADE GRANOLA SNACK BARS

(Adapted from Amanda Love, *A Year of Seasonal Menu Plans*, at thebarefootcook.com)

¼ cup butter, pastured

1 cup raw walnuts, chopped

½ cup raw pecans, chopped

2 ½ cup rolled oats

½ cup raisins

½ cup shredded coconut

1 TSP organic cinnamon

⅔ cup almond butter

⅓ cup honey

⅓ cup maple syrup

1 TBS vanilla extract

Pinch of sea salt

½ cup dark chocolate chips (I like the tiny ones from Enjoy Life)

Melt butter in a small pan. Chop the walnuts and pecans, either in a food processor or by hand. Place the chopped nuts in a large bowl, along with the oats, raisins, shredded coconut, and cinnamon; mix well. Add almond butter, honey, maple syrup, vanilla, and salt to the melted butter; stir until combined. Then pour over the oat mixture and stir well. Last, add the dark chocolate chips. Press the mixture into a glass buttered 9" by 13" dish and refrigerate. After it firms up, cut into small bars as needed.

PEANUT BUTTER COOKIE TREATS

¾ cup butter, softened

1 cup peanut butter (plus extra for filling)

1 cup xylitol (or other healthy sweetener; maple sugar works well)

2 large eggs

1 TBS vanilla extract

2 ½ cups almond flour

¼ TSP sea salt

1 TSP baking soda

Preheat oven to 375 degrees. In the bowl of a mixer, combine butter and peanut butter; mix on high until smooth. Add xylitol and beat until fluffy. Add eggs one at a time, mixing slowly; then add vanilla. Combine dry ingredients in another bowl and then add to wet mixture. Mix just until combined. Using a scoop that yields 2-inch cookies, scoop dough and place on a parchment-lined cookie sheet and gently flatten them. Bake for 8–10 minutes. Once cooled, put a spoonful of peanut butter on the flat side of half the cookies and place remaining cookies on top to make each a cookie sandwich.

LEMON ALMOND COOKIES
(Adapted from elanaspantry.com)

2 cups almond flour
¼ cup butter
¼ cup raw honey
½ TSP vanilla or almond extract
¼ TSP sea salt
Zest of 1 lemon

Preheat oven to 350 degrees. In a medium bowl, combine all ingredients and mix thoroughly with a hand mixer. The dough will look like it's not coming together but stay with it. Drop the batter by rounded tablespoons onto a parchment-lined cookie sheet. Shape into balls and press flat with your fingers. The dough is easier to work with if you place it in the freezer first for 10–20 minutes, but it can be shaped as is—it will just be a little sticky. Bake for 8–10 minutes (these are better undercooked).

Once cooled, prepare the frosting:

2 TBS butter
2 TBS raw honey
½ TSP vanilla or almond extract
Zest of 1 lemon
Pinch of sea salt

Place all ingredients in a small bowl and beat well with a hand mixer until creamy. Use a small knife to frost the cookies.

Beverages

KAVA COLADA*

Add the following ingredients to a Vitamix:

1 can full-fat coconut milk

1 ripe banana

2 heaping cups of frozen pineapple

1 TBS vanilla

6–8 Kava Forte tablets from MediHerb, ground to a powder in a coffee grinder or crushed with a mortar and pestle

*You can also add 1 cup frozen strawberries and/or blueberries for a Berry Kava Colada; during the fall and winter seasons, you can add 1 can organic pumpkin, along with 1–2 TBS pumpkin spice mix.

COCONUT LIME BLUEBERRY SHAKE

1 cup frozen blueberries

1 cup ice cubes

1 frozen banana, in chunks

½ avocado

1 TBS honey

Zest of 1 lime

Fresh juice of 1–2 limes

1 can full-fat coconut milk

Place all ingredients in blender and combine until smooth.

CASHEW CREAMER
2 cups of raw cashews
2 cups water
2 TSPS honey
1 TBS vanilla
½ TSP cinnamon
Pinch of sea salt

Powder cashews in Vitamix. Add water, honey, vanilla, cinnamon and sea salt. Blend until creamy. Pour into a quart glass jar and store in fridge.

PECAN OR ALMOND MILK
2 cups pecans or almonds
3–4 cups water
1 TBS vanilla extract
Pinch of sea salt
Nut milk bag

Begin by blending the nuts and water in a blender or Vitamix. Blend until smooth. Then, pour into a nut milk bag, and holding it over a bowl, squeeze the milk out. Pour into glass jar and add sea salt and vanilla. Shake well. This makes about a quart. Feel free to stretch your nut milk by increasing the water to 4–6 cups (using only 3 cups makes a creamier milk).

Please see my online videos at charlottekikel.com for a cooking demonstration on making these nut milks.

LEMON LIVER FLUSH FROM AMANDA LOVE'S NOURISHING CLEANSE

1 whole organic lemon (or grapefruit or lime)
1 quart filtered water
2 TBS olive oil
1 TSP vanilla extract
5 drops liquid stevia extract

Combine all ingredients in a high-powered blender and blend until smooth and creamy. Strain into a bowl to remove pulp and pour into a quart-sized glass jar, storing in the fridge for future use. I drink ½ quart upon waking and ½ quart before bed. You can stretch it out, however, and just drink 1 cup per day.

I have learned so much from Amanda Love. If you need to broaden your recipes, culinary skills, or knowledge of traditional foods, I encourage you to check out her work at thebarefootcook.com.

NOTES

1   Pressfield, S. (2012). *Turning Pro: Tapping Your Inner Power and Creating Your Life's Work,* p. 103. New York: Black Irish Entertainment.

2   Bell, R. (2012). *Drops Like Stars: A Few Thoughts on Creativity and Suffering,* p. 106. New York: Harper Collins.

3   Enriquez, A., & Frankel, D. S. (2017). Arrhythmogenic effects of energy drinks. *Journal of Cardiovascular Electrophysiology,* June 28(6): 711–717.

4   Conway, P. (2011). The Consultation in Phytotherapy: The Herbal Practitioner's *Approach to the Patient, p. 148. Philadelphia: Churchill Livingstone Elsevier.*

5   Bergner, P. (2014). Systemic inflammation, food intolerance, and autoimmunity. Audio CD: North American Institute of Medical Herbalism.

6   Lustig, R. (2013). *Fat Chance: Beating the Odds Against Sugar, Processed Food, Obesity and Disease.* p. 192. New York: Penguin.

7   Green, J. (2007). *The Male Herbal: The Definitive Health Care Book for Men & Boys,* 2nd ed., pp. 29–30. Berkeley: Crossing Press.

8   Li, F. (2013). Taste perception: From the tongue to the testis. *Molecular Human Reproduction,* Feb. 18, 19(6): 349–360.

9 Randall, D. K. (2012). *Dreamland: Adventures in the Strange Science of Sleep*, pp. 244–245. New York: W.W. Norton & Company.

10 Louv, R. (2012). *The Nature Principle: Reconnecting with Life in a Virtual Age*, p. 29. Chapel Hill: Algonquin Books.

11 Kakkib li'Dthia Warrawee'a. (2002). *There Once Was a Tree Called Deru*, p. 258. Australia: Harper Collins.

12 Hinderberger, P. (2017). Childhood vaccinations: An anthroposophical medical perspective. *Renewal: A Journal for Waldorf Education,* Spring/Summer 26(1): 33.

13 Garbes, A. (2015). The more I learn about breast milk, the more amazed I am. *The Stranger*, Aug. 26. http://www.thestranger.com/features/feature/2015/08/26/22755273/the-more-i-learn-about-breast-milk-the-more-amazed-i-am

14 Moberg, K. U. (2003). *The Oxytocin Factor: Tapping the Hormone of Calm, Love, and Healing*, p. 146. Cambridge: Da Capo Press.

15 Yang, Q. (2011). Gain weight by 'going diet?' Artificial sweeteners and the neurobiology of sugar cravings. *Yale Journal of Biology and Medicine*, June, 83(2): 101–108.

16 Lenoir, M, et al. (2007). Intense sweetness surpasses cocaine reward." *PLoS ONE*, 2(8): e698.

CHARLOTTE KIKEL, MS, is a wife, mother, teacher, herbalist, nutritionist, self-care advocate, and founder of Eat in Peace Wellness Consulting. Her professional practice draws wisdom from personal health breakthroughs, commitment to ongoing education, formal training and clinical work. She holds a Masters of Science in Western Herbal Medicine from Maryland University of Integrative Health (formerly the Tai Sophia Institute) and is a graduate of the Nutrition Consultant program at Bauman College in Santa Cruz, California. She lives in Austin, Texas with her husband and son.

78414890R00188

Made in the USA
Lexington, KY
10 January 2018